# Awakening the Spark Within

## THE TEACHINGS OF KABBALAH SERIES

by Rabbi Yitzchak Ginsburgh
(in English)

*The Hebrew Letters*
*The Mystery of Marriage*
*Awakening the Spark Within*

Coming Soon:

*To Sweeten the Bitter*

# Awakening the Spark Within

## Five Dynamics of Leadership That Can Change the World

Rabbi Yitzchak Ginsburgh

**Linda Pinsky Publications**

*a division of* Gal Einai
*Jerusalem*

Printed in Israel
First Edition

THE TEACHINGS OF KABBALAH SERIES

*Special thanks to* **Rabbi Avraham Arieh Trugman** *for the hundreds of hours he spent painstakingly nurturing this book from its infancy into its present form.*

edited by U. Obst

For information address:

USA:   Gal Einai Institute, Inc.
       PO Box 41
       Cedarhurst, NY 11516-9862,
       tel/fax (toll-free): (888) 453-0571

Israel:  Gal Einai
       PO Box 1015
       Kefar Chabad 72915
       tel.: (02) 996-1123; fax: (02) 996-2111

E-mail:  inner@inner.org.

Web:    www.inner.org

Gal Einai publishes and produces books, pamphlets, audiocassettes and videocassettes by Rabbi Yitzchak Ginsburgh. To receive a catalog of our products in English and/or Hebrew, please contact us at any of the above addresses, email orders@inner.org, or visit www.inner-store.org.

*For behold, darkness shall cover the earth...*
*Nations shall then go by Your light*
*and kings by Your radiant illumination.*

—Isaiah 60:2-3

This book is dedicated
to my beautiful parents

Maurice

and

Suzanne

# Suissa

# Table of Contents

# Introduction

## THE VISION

Of the millions of words recorded over time describing a perfect world of peace, brotherhood and harmony, perhaps none speak more eloquently than these:

> And they shall beat their swords into plowshares and their spears into pruning hooks; nation shall not lift up sword against nation, neither shall they learn war anymore... [At that time] the wolf shall dwell with the lamb, the leopard lie down with the kid, the calf and the beast of prey shall feed together with a little child to herd them.[1]

These words belong to the Jewish prophet Isaiah. They describe what all humanity yearns for, a vision of the perfect future—a future without war, without hunger, without strife.

This vision is better known as the Messianic vision, because it is expected to become reality upon the coming of the Messiah, the Anointed One, the Great Peacemaker, the Ultimate Leader.[2]

1

At the present moment, this vision seems very far from ever coming true. And yet the Bible says that it is not only possible, but possible now![3] And furthermore, that it is the primary responsibility of the Jewish people to bring this vision about.[4] This is why in Isaiah's prophecy Israel is called a "light unto the nations."[5]

It is an awesome responsibility, because it means no less than leading the world to its ultimate fulfillment.

But how?

How can an average Jew—who perhaps is worried about his or her next paycheck, the state of his health, or the lack of values her children are exposed to daily—even begin to contemplate such an awesome task?

The answer, which will be examined in depth in this book, can be summed up simply: by cultivating, in everyday personal life, his or her own innate leadership qualities. Modest as the effects of this effort may seem, they will ripple out into the collective unconscious of one's community, eventually transform the Jewish people, and then ultimately change the world. When the stage is thus set, the Ultimate Leader will emerge to fulfill the hopes of all good people.

Presently, there is no doubt that the world is waiting for true leadership, poised, as it is, on the brink of chaos.


# An Ancient Prediction


The *Zohar*, the classic text of Kabbalah composed nearly two thousand years ago, predicted the advances in civilization that would precipitate this state of affairs in our day and age.[6] It states that in "the six-hundredth year of the sixth millennium"[7] the "lower waters" of knowledge would burst forth throughout the world. The six-hundredth year of the sixth millennium corresponds roughly to the beginning of the scientific and industrial revolutions and the myriad of changes they have wrought in their wake.[8]

Indeed, the radical changes in lifestyle and the revolutionary advances in science, medicine, communications, and government in the last 150 years have truly "flooded" and overwhelmed traditional morals and values without regard to national borders, religion, or culture. The world is being transformed at such an astounding speed that nations and individuals are at a loss to adjust to constantly changing reality.

We face a crisis situation at all levels of society; wherever we look we see dysfunction, instability, turmoil, apathy, confusion.

At the crux is a crisis in leadership and the concurrent weakening of morals and ethics.

It is unclear whether the lack of leadership is the cause of the general weakening of society's moral fiber, or whether the disintegration of stable institutions and the subsequent weakening of ethics have caused a vacuum in leadership. No matter what the source of the problem, it is obvious that traditional leadership roles have lost much of their power and respect.

Corruption in the highest ranks of almost every nation on the globe has left the world largely cynical and skeptical about leadership in general.[9] Not only has this disillusionment with leadership poisoned people's attitudes about today's leaders (or possible leaders), it has caused them to suspect the great leaders of the past as well. The world no longer believes in heroes or true leadership, and this loss of faith has opened up a huge void that seemingly no single individual could ever fill.

In the Jewish world, the acute lack of leadership is felt as a result of an additional reason—the devastation of the Holocaust. The murder of six million Jews and the wholesale destruction of thousands of established communities and institutions have wreaked such havoc that its effects continue to be felt to this day.

And yet darkness is always juxtaposed with light in Jewish history.

One of the most significant contributions of the Jewish people has been its ability to inspire the world at large. Many religions, philosophies, social causes, political movements and artistic endeavors throughout the ages have drawn sustenance from the Bible (the Five Books of Moses, the Prophets, and the Writings). Although this fact is largely forgotten today, the values that are now inseparably linked with just government based on human rights and dignity came from the Five Books of Moses, the Torah. The ideas of love, brotherhood, justice, equality, peace, compassion, social responsibility, kindness to strangers and the poor, holiness of human purpose, reverence for life, and self-discipline, *all* have their origin in the teachings of the Torah, which broke all precedents when it first emerged in the ancient world. And, from it, too, came the ideas of how the world can be changed for the better—what Kabbalah calls *tikun olam*—how the world can be rectified and brought toward the universal vision of redemption. That this will eventually take place we know from the Jewish prophets: Isaiah, Jeremiah, Ezekiel, Micah and others.

The prophecy of Isaiah is outstanding in this regard—his words of salvation and consolation reverberate throughout the generations.

At the same time, the writings of Isaiah (as well as the other prophets) contain dire warnings and threats of terrible consequences should society ignore the principles of loving-kindness, peace, and justice.

The first chapter of the Book of Isaiah, which opens with the words, "the vision of Isaiah…," is traditionally read[10] in synagogues on the "Shabbat of Vision" which, in the Hebrew calendar, immediately precedes the 9th day of the month of *Av*. The 9th of *Av*—*Tisha B'Av*—is the catastrophic day in Jewish history when the First Temple was destroyed by the Babylonians; when the Second Temple was destroyed by the Romans; when the Jews of Spain were given an ultimatum by the Inquisition—leave, convert, or die; when World War I, the prelude to the Holocaust, began; and when many other calamities were visited upon the Jewish people. It is at a time of the remembrance of such terrible darkness that the vision of Isaiah is also recalled.

It begins with chilling words, as the prophet describes the sad state of affairs in Israel of his time, but it ends with words of consolation, a promise of hope and redemption.

## OUT OF DESTRUCTION

We can infer from this that a Jewish vision of redemption is one that ultimately emanates out of destruction. For this reason the "Shabbat of Vision" precedes the 9th of *Av*—in order that the vision of future redemption can combat, neutralize and ultimately vanquish the destructive forces concentrated on this fateful day.

Similarly, standing on the brink of chaos, a true visionary has the ability to see a glorious future.

This idea is embodied in the statement of the sages who teach that this True Visionary, the Ultimate Leader, the Messiah, will be born on the 9$^{th}$ of *Av*. He will be conceived in the collective super-conscious of the Jewish people and his birth will be the manifestation of the deeply held belief in the ultimate redemption of the world.

Even now, at a time of such great turmoil, we have a sense that the utopian vision of which the world dreams is just around the corner, and that, if we could but pull the curtain back, we would see it advancing toward us.

The Talmudic answer to the question, "Who is Wise?"— "He who sees what is [to be] born"[11]—can be understood as: "He who sees all the potential in the present moment and how it will actualize in the future."[12]

Although there may be no prophets walking the earth today, each person retains the potential glimmer of prophecy deep within his or her soul. Indeed, a vision of the ultimate future can only be grasped through our present reality; and it can be actualized by each one of us through the dynamics of leadership as outlined by the Kabbalah. These dynamics of leadership are potent tools for contacting deeply dormant powers of the soul, enabling us to manifest the redemptive process as an essential part of our everyday lives, and, in so doing, to bring the future into the present.

This book was written with the current crisis in mind. Unlike many books on the subject of leadership, the emphasis here is not on external skills, strategies, or techniques of political manipulation, but rather on the Kabbalistic and Hassidic view of the inner qualities needed to nurture and develop authentic Jewish leadership—on the personal level, on the community level, within the nation of Israel, and worldwide. This perspective presents an antidote to a major aspect of the present leadership crisis—namely, the overemphasis on, and even an obsession with, superficial appearances and power games, and disregard for tangible manifestation of true leadership qualities.

We will first look at the general nature of leadership as it is understood in Jewish mystical writings, and then go on to examine in depth the five dynamics or inherent qualities of leadership and how we can apply them in our lives.

It is our sincere hope that, once empowered with this knowledge, the reader will be inspired to act within his or her sphere of influence to create meaningful contributions, however small, to the awesome task of realizing the ultimate vision for the world. For as Hillel, the great teacher of two thousand years ago, said: "If not now, when?"[13]

# 1

# Leadership Defined

## CARRYING THE WORLD

Among the great allegorical classics of the Hassidic tradition is the story of "The Seven Beggars," told by Rabbi Nachman of Breslov,[1] and widely considered his masterpiece. It is a mystical tale of two small children, a boy and a girl, separated from their parents in the midst of war. Lost in the woods, hungry and desperate, they encounter seven beggars who feed and comfort them. One of the beggars is blind, the second deaf, the third stammers, the fourth has a crooked neck, the fifth is a hunchback, the sixth has no hands, and the seventh has no feet. Each beggar, before he leaves the children, blesses them that they might become like him.

Eventually, the children find their way out of the woods; years pass and when they decide to marry, the beggars of the kingdom organize a wedding feast in their honor. Over the seven days of rejoicing, the seven beggars from the forest return and now announce their intention to complete the blessing that each had bestowed long ago—what was potential then is to be actualized now.

Each beggar then reveals that his apparent physical disability is only superficial and, in fact, is a source of great spiritual strength.

When the fifth beggar, the hunchback, arrives, he announces:

"When you were little children, I blessed you with a wish that you would be like me. Now I grant you this as my wedding gift to you. I am not a hunchback at all. The reason I appear to be so is because my shoulders are 'the little that holds much,' and I shall tell you how I know this to be true."

He then tells a story of a group of people who searched in vain for the way to a tree in whose shade every animal would want to lie and in whose branches every bird would want to find shelter. The people knew such a tree existed, and that birds and animals of every kind lived there, all mingling and playing together and never harming each other. They desired very much to go to that tree, for they realized that such a tree must surely be in Paradise. But no matter how they tried to get there, they kept getting lost.

Then they learned from a wise man that only those who were like the tree could reach the tree, for the roots of the tree were faith in God, awe of God, and humility; and its trunk was truth. So the people worked very hard to improve themselves and develop these traits until they were finally ready. They set out together and, after a lengthy journey, they saw the tree from afar. And that is when they realized that the tree did not grow in soil; it existed in another dimension altogether. But if the tree existed in a realm that was beyond space, how could they reach it? They were dismayed until the beggar, who was with them, said that he could carry them all to the tree on his back.

"I could bring them to the tree which is beyond space," explained the beggar, "for I exist at the threshold between space and that which is beyond space. I brought them to the tree, and that is how I know that my shoulders are 'the little that holds much.'"

And so the beggar blessed the newlyweds that they should be like him and carry the world on their back to another, higher dimension.

Each generation has its hunchback beggar—a leader capable of carrying the world on his shoulder to the Tree of Life[2]—the place of redemption—where there is only peace and brotherhood and love, and where the wolf lies down with the lamb. But the leader can only do so if the rest of us are willing to take the journey beyond our present reality, toward the vision of the future.

If we do, the leader becomes a bridge between this world and the future order that the prophecies describe.

When we examine these prophecies, we see that they paint a picture of a world that is similar to ours in some ways but radically different in others[3]—a picture of a world operating within dimensions of reality that we cannot readily grasp with our limited intellects.

To take Isaiah's famous prophecy as an example, we can imagine nations signing disarmament treaties and agreeing not to wage war anymore. It may be a far-fetched dream, but it could conceivably happen without requiring any supernatural alteration of reality. But in order for the wolf to lie down with the lamb, some fundamental change in the nature of reality will have to occur that will alter the way wolves and lambs think and behave. Familiar as this image of peacefulness is, in order for it to become real, the world will have to function in a whole new way.

Although, at present, our world appears to be three-dimensional, we can nevertheless live with an awareness that there exist other levels of reality beyond what our physical senses can immediately detect. The closer we examine the prophecies about these other levels of reality, the closer we come to this utopian world of the future which is meant to sprout out of our chaotic present.

Each one of us has the capacity right now to reveal the World to Come as a world that is already becoming.[4] By pioneering new models of understanding, based on the prophetic visions of the future, and improving the world within the purview of our influence, we become active agents of redemption.

We have the ability to connect with the future and to envision the Ultimate Leader who will bring it about because each one of us has a spark of the Ultimate Leader deep within. We can have a vision of the future, because it is already contained in us. (Indeed, this is one of the key teachings of the Ba'al Shem Tov, the great 18th century teacher and founder of the Hassidic movement.)[5]

Ultimately, we are all responsible to do everything we can to ignite that inner spark. Thus we can inspire others as well, carrying them to new heights of awareness and empowering that one person among us who—like the beggar—could take us to heretofore unreachable levels.

According to Jewish tradition, there is one individual in every generation who has the potential to be the Ultimate Leader. He encompasses the total, inclusive consciousness of all the myriad sparks that are present in his generation. He awakens and enlivens within as many individuals as possible a spiritual vision, which in turn affects the entire world. Thus, each generation makes its unique contribution, paving the way for the ultimate redemption.

A potential Ultimate Leader attempts to unite everyone together, taking upon himself the awesome weight of responsibility of the entire people. According to the merit of his generation, he manages to accomplish at least part of his mission.

An individual and generation will arise in the future that will succeed in this endeavor and, finally, the entire task will be completed. Only then will we understand the total historical process—how each person, generation, and particular leader contributed his or her unique piece to the overall puzzle, until the final, complete picture emerges in all its pristine grandeur.

The unique ability and task of the potential Ultimate Leader, is thus to lift his generation to a state of transcendence above the limitations of time and space. This he can best do with the power of his words, and with the power of his silence. In order for his speech to reflect his silence, and his silence to speak, he must be truly humble. Humbleness, especially as experienced in heartfelt prayer to God, links silence to speech.

We will now examine these three general qualities of leadership—speech, humbleness, and silence—and how they enable the leader to establish a true union between himself and his followers.[6] Inasmuch as all of these qualities are reflected in speech, they may all be seen as levels of speech:

- expressive, explicit speech

- humble, quiet speech

- silent speech—the "still, silent voice" which the prophet Elijah heard when he fled into the wilderness[7]

# THE POWER OF SPEECH

The sages declare, "There is but one leader of a generation, not two leaders of a generation,"[8] and in so doing use the word *dabar* which means "leader" but, more specifically, "spokesman." Thus, we learn that the sense of speech—and its ability to affect the world—lies at the foundation of the Jewish view of leadership.

The fact that a leader derives his authority from his power of speech is expressed in many places in the Bible. For example, King Solomon says in Ecclesiastes, "For the word of the king is authority."[9]

A further connection between speech and leadership is found in the *Zohar*,[10] where each of the ten *sefirot*—the Divine channels through which God creates and relates to the world—is identified by a physical idiom best describing its essence. The last of the ten *sefirot* is *malchut* ("kingship"), which is referred to as *malchut peh*, literally meaning, "kingship is the mouth."

The Book of Genesis lists ten instances when God spoke and an aspect of the creation came into being.[11] And the Divine power to create through speech is mirrored in man, who is created "in the image of God."[12]

> And God formed man from the dust of the earth and breathed into his nostrils the breath of life; and man became a living soul. [13]

The Aramaic translation of the Hebrew for "a living soul" is "a speaking spirit,"[14] which further emphasizes that it is the ability to speak that ultimately separates man from all other living creatures. Along with the gift of speech comes the responsibility to rule:

> And God blessed them and God said to them, "Be fruitful and multiply, replenish the earth and subdue it, and have dominion over the fish of the sea and over the birds of the sky and over every living thing that moves on the earth."[15]

Created in the image of God, human beings were endowed with the power that brought creation into being—God's metaphoric faculty of speech, which is one and the same as His power of action. This unique gift is mirrored in our ability to affect our surrounding reality—for positive or negative—through speech. We have all experienced words that wound; an inspiring speech that changed our moods, attitudes, or, at times, our entire lives; or a verbal command by an authority figure that established immediate order out of chaos.

The Talmud, recognizing the power of speech, describes one who embarrasses another in public as nothing less than a "murderer,"[16] while the sages point out numerous violations of Torah law caused by *lashon hara*, literally "evil speech," meaning speech that is derogatory of others.[17] Choosing our words carefully in order to promote good and not cause harm, and being mindful and sincere in their delivery, is seen by Judaism as fundamental.

The direct connection between the power of speech and leadership is manifest today to a degree greater than perhaps at any other time in history due to technological advances and the media. Never has an individual had at his or her disposal the opportunity to address such a wide audience so quickly and at such frequency. If we understand all communication to be an extension of speech,

then today's common access to television, instantaneous satellite
news coverage, E-mail, and the Internet has presented the world
with an unprecedented opportunity for widely effective leadership,
cooperation, problem-solving, and harmony. A shallow concept
of leadership, however, can engender the misuse of these powerful
communication tools to the detriment of all humanity. History
testifies how one man in Germany, through his mesmerizing use
of speech and propaganda, was able to wreak worldwide havoc,
wipe out a third of the Jewish people, and plunge the world into a
spiritual abyss from which it is still trying to recover. In
contemporary politics, this pattern is repeating itself as in-depth
treatment of complex issues is being replaced by catchwords and
slogans in response to media that feed on multi-second sound
bites.

Another connection between speech and leadership is
found in one of the most ancient texts of Kabbalah, *Sefer Yetzirah*.[18]
Among other mystical concepts, the book deals with the twenty-
two Hebrew letters, which it describes as the building blocks of
creation, and which it divides into sub-groups based on both
grammatical and spiritual considerations.[19]

Each letter in the sub-group of the twelve "simple" letters
is seen as the spiritual source associated with one of the twelve
months of the year, as well as one of the twelve tribes of Israel.
*Sefer Yetzirah* further identifies each letter with a specific "sense" in
the soul and a certain limb or organ of the body that directs that
sense.

The first of the simple letters is the letter *hei*. It is the
spiritual source associated with *Nissan*, the month of Passover,
when the Jewish people were freed from Egyptian bondage, and
with the tribe of Judah, blessed by both Jacob and Moses to be the

leader of all the tribes. It is from Judah that future kings would arise, most specifically King David and his lineage. Its sense in the soul is speech, while its "leading" limb is the right foot, alluding to the forward thrust inherent in leadership.

An allusion to speech is contained in the name of Judah— in Hebrew *Yehudah*, the root of which is *hod*, a word of multiple meanings each connected to an aspect of speech. Depending on its context, *hod* can mean "praise," "acknowledgment," "confession," "thanks," "echo," or "glory." Judah received his name from his mother Leah, as the Torah relates:

> She conceived again and gave birth to a son. She said, "This time I will praise [*odeh*] God." She therefore named him Judah [*Yehudah*].[20]

The ability to praise and acknowledge comprises the basic attitude reflected in the Psalms of David and in all subsequent formal prayers as formulated by the sages.[21]

An additional aspect of acknowledgment, connected to another meaning of *hod*, is the ability to admit or to confess misdeeds and shortcomings.

The defining moment in the life of Judah was the drama involving his daughter-in-law Tamar. Twice widowed and denied by Judah marriage to his third son, Tamar posed as a prostitute and seduced Judah himself. Then, pregnant, she silently faced death for adultery, rather than embarrass him. Finally realizing that he was the father, Judah confessed his mistake by publicly declaring, "She is more righteous than I."[22]

Through his admission of guilt, Judah became the first person in the Torah to accept responsibility for misdeed willingly, thereby becoming the archetypal example of sincere and wholehearted repentance. His descendant King David likewise had the strength of character to acknowledge personal failings in an incident involving the pregnant Bathsheba. When confronted by the prophet Nathan with his deeds—which included sending Bathsheba's husband, Uriah, to the battlefront where Uriah met his death—David openly declared, "I have sinned to God."[23]

From this line of great leaders, who were capable of the greatest humility before God, will eventually come the Ultimate Leader, *Mashiach ben David*, "the Messiah, son of David," who will lead the world to true unity in the consciousness of God.


When applied to speech, the different meanings of *hod*— "acknowledgment," "praise," "thanks," "echo," "confession," and "glory"—relate to another of the central teachings of the Ba'al Shem Tov. He taught that Divine consciousness is achieved through a three-stage process of spiritual growth:[24]

- "submission"
- "separation"
- "sweetening"

The first stage of spiritual growth, that of "submission," corresponds to the aspects of *hod* discussed above—praise, echo, acknowledgment, thanksgiving, and confession—all of which depend on accepting the reality of a higher force that leads our lives and recognizing the need to adjust our behavior appropriately.

"Separation" is the second stage of spiritual growth, where God's law plays a decisive role in directing all of one's thoughts, speech, and actions.[25] When we separate ourselves from the transitory and mundane and immerse ourselves in the Torah, then even speech relating to the mundane aspects of life can be infused with spirituality and may serve as an example to others.[26] Here *hod* acknowledges the ultimate truth of the Torah and fully identifies with its way of life, as echoed in every utterance of one's mouth.

The culminating stage of spiritual growth is "sweetening." This relates to the most common translation of *hod*—"glory," as in "the glory of kingship."[27] The level of speech alluded to here is speech that "leads" by elevating and inspiring others. Such speech reflects the Divine creative process and the power to sweeten reality.[28]

Although *Mashiach ben David* is expected to be both a military and political leader, he will ultimately conquer the world through speech: by illuminating all of Israel and the world with the light of Torah.

At that time, the prophecy of Zephaniah of 2,600 years ago will be fulfilled:

> "For then I will convert the nations to speak a pure language, so that they may all proclaim the Name of God, to serve Him with a united resolve. "[29]

## THE MIGHT OF HUMILITY

It is a paradox that the more one is aware of becoming a conduit for God's will—that is, the more humble one becomes—the greater one's leadership ability. This is because the more one rectifies the ego, the more one empowers the soul. And the way to a rectified ego is, of course, a connection with God. As the great 3rd century sage Rabban Gamliel teaches:

> Make His will as your will, that He may make your will as His will. Nullify your will to His will, that He may nullify the will of others to your will.[30]

The central word representing the self—"I"—appears in many verses relating to both ego and leadership.

Adonijah, the son of King David, who wanted to assume the monarchy while his father was still alive and the acknowledged ruler, began his "campaign" with the statement, "I shall rule."[31] In Kabbalah, this statement is viewed as the quintessential example of unrectified ego. King David, on the other hand, said of himself, with total humility, "poor and desolate am I."[32]

Interestingly, in Hebrew, the words "poor" and "I" are pronounced alike (*ani*) but one is spelled with the letter *ayin* and the other with the letter *alef*, which phonetically are very similar and in many instances interchangeable. Therefore, when King David says, "poor...am I," the letter *ayin* of the word for "poor" is transformed into the letter *alef* of the word for "I." From this we learn that the process leading to a rectified ego occurs through an existential sense of lowliness and spiritual poverty.

Another allusion to the idea of clarified self-consciousness is found by permuting the letters of the word *ani*, "I," (*alef-nun-yud*) to spell the word *ayin*, "nothing," (*alef-yud-nun*). One of the most basic Jewish beliefs is that God created the world *ex nihilo*, "something from nothing," which, as explained in mystical teachings, is not an event that occurred once in the distant past, but is rather a continuous Divine act that sustains all of reality. Experiencing continuous re-creation from an infinite, all-knowing Creator rectifies one's ego and cultivates leadership qualities in one's soul.

Of God the Creator, it is said in the Talmud:

> In every place that you find the greatness of God, there will you find His humility.[33]

The greatness of creation reflects God's infinite humility to "lower" His infinite essence to involve Himself, as it were, with finite reality. Just as God Himself is humble, how much more so should this hold true for a human being created "in the image of God." Humility reflects Godliness and prepares one for leadership.

According to Kabbalah and Hassidism, the essential rectification of ego occurs through heartfelt prayer. This is alluded to in King David's statement: "I am prayer,"[34] which may be understood to imply, "the rectification of my 'I,' my ego, is through prayer."

Prayer in Judaism is therefore envisioned as enveloping and affecting the individual's entire being. Thus, the *Amidah*, the prayer of silent devotion, is divided into three sections, each section corresponding to a different fundamental attitude deemed necessary for prayer to reflect a true, existential relationship with God: praise, request, and thanks. In addition, we are taught that our prayers of silent devotion should not be totally inward, but should be articulated ever so quietly (by the movement of the lips), thereby transmuting thought into breath—which is the origin of speech—and into action.[35]

The statement of the sages, "Would it only be that a person would pray all day,"[36] reflects not the desire that one should remain in the synagogue all day praying, but that one's world view, which informs all one's daily activities, should emanate from the continuous state of humility and closeness to God that prayer engenders.

Paradoxically, the Hebrew word for "lowliness" (*shefel*) is numerically equal to the word for "pride" (*gei'ut*).[37] In Hebrew, these terms also stand for "low tide" and "high tide," which are equal and complement one another. Ego and pride, when clarified and rectified, give power to an individual—especially a leader—to initiate and inspire.

When speech and ego are purified through prayer, what follows is the awakening of compassion and commitment from on high, as well as from within, to bring salvation to the world. This is expressed in the words of Isaiah:

> I [who] speak with righteousness, am mighty to save.[38]

## THE STRENGTH OF SILENCE

The fourth of the Five Books of Moses is commonly called Numbers (due to the census that begins it), but in Hebrew this book is known as *Bamidbar*, which literally means "in the desert." It is fascinating to note that the root of the word for "desert" (*midbar*) is *daber*, which means "speech," and that one of the recurring themes of the Book of *Bamidbar* is the ongoing leadership struggle—the dialogues and debates—which took place throughout the forty years the Jews wandered in the desert.

And yet, paradoxically, when envisioning a desert, one usually thinks of a great barren expanse and penetrating silence.

Jacob, Moses, and David were all leaders of the Jewish people who cultivated their innate potential for leadership while tending their flocks in the meditative quiet of the desert. Many of the prophets, as well, found the desert silence the perfect environment for prophetic experience.

An allusion to the silence which precedes, and leads to, the potent speech of a leader is contained in the most mysterious word of the Bible—*chashmal*—used by the prophet Ezekiel to describe his astounding vision of the chariot:

> And I looked, and behold, a storm wind came
> out of the north, a great cloud and a fire flaring
> up and a brightness was about it, like *chashmal*,
> out of the midst of the fire.[39]

*Chashmal* is most often translated as the "color of electrum" or the "color of amber," but the sages understood that *chashmal* was not just a color but an energy, and indeed modern Hebrew translates it as "electricity." Dividing *chashmal* into syllables produces two antithetical concepts—"silence" (*chash*) and "speaking" (*mal*). This suggests that a state of rectified speech follows the quiet, meditative preparation of silence. On an even deeper level it describes a simultaneous state of "silence" within speech, and "speech" within silence.[40]

The idea of speech within silence is illustrated in the life of another prophet, Elijah. Fleeing the wrath of King Ahab and his wife Jezebel, whose evil ways he had condemned, Elijah reached the desert of Sinai. And it is there that he had an encounter with God, described in an unforgettable passage in the Book of Kings:

> And behold, God passed by, and a great and
> strong wind rent the mountains and broke the
> rocks in pieces before God, but God was not in
> the wind. And after the wind—an earthquake,
> but God was not in the earthquake. And after
> the earthquake—a fire, but God was not in the
> fire. And after the fire—a still silent voice. And
> when Elijah heard it he wrapped his face in a
> mantle and went out and stood in the entrance
> of the cave. And then a voice addressed him,
> "What are you doing here, Elijah?"[41]

This "silent" voice is the manner in which God speaks to each and every person, according to his or her readiness to hear His personal message.

Elijah's experience with the still, silent voice of God occurred in the desert, a place where God, in many cases, reveals Himself to the potential and sometimes unsuspecting leader. This is the place where the leader first comes face to face with the task before him—the mission that is uniquely his.

Conceptually, the desert represents the mental space wherein the spark of leadership, dormant within each individual, has the opportunity, like a desert plant, to grow despite the forbidding environment. The desert provides a natural atmosphere of separation and isolation. It provides space for contemplation and meditation, the silence needed before the leader is revealed— first to himself and God—and only later to his people.[42]

The phenomenon of a future leader experiencing a period of "dormancy" or "silence," only later to step into his role, is present in some degree in the stories of almost all Biblical heroes—most dramatically with Moses and David. Their stories illustrate an important facet of leadership—a call to action. God seeks out a leader for His people and challenges him to lead.

In the case of David, God commanded the prophet Samuel to find a replacement for King Saul, who had not followed God's orders regarding the war with the nation of Amalek:

> And God said to Samuel: "How long will you mourn for Saul seeing I have rejected him from reigning over Israel. Fill your horn with oil and go, I will send you to Jesse of Bethlehem, for I have provided for Me a king among his sons."[43]

In the case of Moses, the dialogue at the burning bush stands out as a prime example of God appointing an initially resistant individual to assume a public role.

> "Now go, I am sending you to Pharaoh, and you will bring My people, the children of Israel, out of Egypt." Moses said to God, "Who am I that I should go to Pharaoh? Am I able to bring the children of Israel out of Egypt?"[44]

This, in itself, points to a further paradox—the prototype of the Jewish leader as an introverted person, who by nature shies away from taking center stage. It is precisely this type of individual, who does not seek fame or glory, that God chooses to lead.

The comparison of this model of leadership with the model of modern society is striking. Today, one seeking to lead studies political science or goes into politics as a profession, sharpening those skills that will allow him or her to compete in the world of money and power. In Jewish thought, leadership is a

responsibility that one may need to assume, but it is never a means
to fulfill a need for power or self-aggrandizement.

King Solomon was only twelve years old when he assumed
the throne as successor to his father, King David. Shortly after,
God appeared to him in a dream in which He invited Solomon to
make a request for himself. Solomon answered:

> "And now my God, You have made your
> servant king instead of David my father, and I
> am but a small child.... Give, therefore, your
> servant an understanding heart to judge your
> people..." And God said, "Because you have
> not requested riches and honor but only that
> which would benefit all the people, I will give
> you not only an understanding heart like none
> other before or after you...but also riches and
> honor like no other king in your days."[45]

The sages confirm in many statements that honor eludes
one who aggressively pursues it and crowns the one who does his
best to avoid the illusionary trappings of power. If a person is truly
destined or fitting for leadership, then opportunities will present
themselves in a natural and organic way.[46]

This contrasts sharply with the manner in which, for
example, the Communists came to power in Russia in 1917. While
they represented numerically only the smallest of ideological
minorities, they seized power and imposed a seventy-year, iron-
fisted reign over their entire region. Any regime that comes to
power in such an unnatural way is bound to eventually collapse
under its own self-imposed delusions of grandeur.

The historical dynamic as just described mirrors a much deeper reality. Kabbalah speaks of a state/world of "chaos" (*tohu*) preceding the state/world of "rectification" (*tikun*). According to the Ari,[47] the great 16th century Kabbalist, this first world broke apart due to the inability of its vessels to contain and mutually share the Divine light flowing into them, thereby causing their own destruction. The mystics find a parallel to this idea in the Book of Genesis[48] where eight Edomite kings are named "who ruled before a king ruled in Israel"; after the name of each king it states, "he ruled and he died." According to Kabbalah, these kings represent the "breaking of the vessels" in the world of chaos. Similarly, false leaders and ideologies eventually "break" and fade away. Only concerning the last king, Hadar, does it state that "he ruled" but not that "he died." Hadar alludes to the beginning of the world of rectification.[49]

While the potential for true and authentic leadership presents itself repeatedly throughout the Bible (and indeed, a number of honest, God-fearing leaders rose to the challenge), generally, the rulers we find described there were egocentric and destructive individuals lacking the most fundamental prerequisite of leadership—submission to God's will. The final result of unrectified leadership was the destruction of the Temple and the exile of the Jewish people.

Of all the kings of Israel, it is King David who shines forth as the paradigm of a true Jewish leader. Even his shortcomings and trials bring out redeeming factors worthy of emulation. Only to David did God promise an everlasting kingdom and only from his line will the Ultimate Leader, the Messiah, sprout forth.

Deep within the complex nature of the soul of David lies a simple, all-encompassing submission to God. From that undiluted point, the composite soul of Israel is vividly expressed through the rectified speech of David, as revealed in the Book of Psalms, the crowning legacy given to the world by the "sweet singer of Israel."[50] In the future it will be *Mashiach ben David* who shall sing the tenth and final archetypal song of creation—"a new song to God."[51]

## THE UNION

The capacity to lead rests ultimately upon the feeling of the leader's followers that he reflects their conscious and unconscious dreams, aspirations and beliefs. An essential spiritual bonding occurs between the leader and each of his followers. More than a mere state of identification, the union of leader and followers opens new vistas and dimensions within the souls of both.

The Hebrew word for "king" (*melech*) contains within it the word for "speaking" (*mal*) and the word for "going" (*lech*). This alludes to the teaching of *Sefer Yetzirah* quoted above that the right foot "leads" the sense of speech and corresponds to Judah, the tribe of kingship. The purpose of a leader is to lead, to take his people somewhere they would not be able to reach on their own.

The Book of Numbers tells the story of Korach, who attempted to overthrow Moses and Aaron as leaders of the people.[52] Although the story begins: "And Korach took..." what follows gives no indication of what he "took," or where exactly he "took" his followers.[53] The sages interpret this to mean that Korach "took" the people through his charismatic speech. Moses, on the other hand, had a physical speech impediment, which, interestingly enough, was turned to an advantage—whenever Moses addressed the people flawlessly, it was clear that the Divine Presence was speaking through him.[54]

In the Talmud, a series of prophetic predictions are given regarding events that will occur before the coming of the Messiah. One of these "signs" is that the preceding generation will have "a face like a dog,"[55] meaning that its leadership will, in some way, resemble a dog. One interpretation of this analogy is that a dog always runs ahead of his master appearing to lead, but always looks back to his master to get a sign as to which direction he should take. This analogy describes most of today's so-called leaders who lead only in appearance, forever looking behind at the press and public opinion polls to gauge which opinions to adopt.

Within this negative phenomenon is actually hidden a positive aspect if properly understood and applied. A true leader also "looks back," in a sense, but for different reasons. He not only leads but is forever "looking back" to God—the source of his mission—for instruction as to which direction to pursue.[56] In addition, a compassionate leader is always "looking back" to his generation, forever strengthening the soul-connection between them and himself, and never demanding of them more than they can carry.

The most telling sign of a good leader is whether his people are joyous and content. The Hebrew letters of the word *Mashiach*, when re-arranged, spell the word for "will gladden" (*yesamach*). At the conclusion of the dedication of the Temple by King Solomon, the Bible relates:

> On the eighth day he sent away the people and they blessed the king and went to their tents joyful and glad of heart for all the goodness that God had done for David His servant and for Israel His people.[57]

It is not a coincidence that the people rejoiced on the eighth day. The number eight signifies a level of consciousness above nature and logic. The bond between the people and their ruler transcends all other relationships, touching the deepest super-conscious point of the soul,[58] the origin point of the spark of the Messiah, the Ultimate Leader, within each individual Jewish soul. The sense of joy emanating from the soul-union of leader and people creates an experience of redemption and new life.

This is described by Isaiah as the passionate yearning "to see the king in his glory."[59] The phenomenon of movie stars, rock stars, and sports figures drawing huge, occasionally even near-hysterical, crowds is but a perverted shadow of this reality.

The story of creation begins with the Hebrew word *bereshit*, commonly translated as "in the beginning." Whenever this word appears in the Bible subsequently, it is always in conjunction with the beginning of the reign of a Jewish ruler. In a time to come, we will again hear this word, signaling the arrival of the Ultimate Leader. The Messianic era will truly be a new beginning, infusing all of reality with a new life force and the exhilaration of true and complete redemption.

# THE FIVE DYNAMICS OF LEADERSHIP

Having defined the concept of leadership in broad general terms, we will now explore five specific dynamics of leadership.[60] The qualities of leadership that will be discussed are not external Machiavellian manifestations of power politics, but rather inner, soul properties of spiritual refinement. These five dynamics have been identified through an intense investigation of the subject of leadership as it is treated in the full spectrum of ancient sources and more contemporary commentaries. Specifically, the mystical tradition—as revealed in Kabbalah and Hassidism—serves as the main source of inspiration.

The five dynamics of leadership which we will be exploring in detail are:

1. The Art of Compromise

2. The Drive for Wholeness

3. The Power of Compassion to Inspire

4. The Drive for Integration

5. A Sense of Folly

Our sincere desire in this exploration is not merely to bring certain ideas to light, but to inspire the reader to search for and find the sparks of leadership within himself or herself.[61]

Complete redemption will come when enough individual sparks of the Ultimate Leader, the Messiah, are ignited and activated in the world. May we all merit to see a "new light shine on Zion," [62] speedily in our days.

# 2

# First Dynamic

## THE ART OF COMPROMISE

The first prerequisite of leadership is the ability of the leader to find favor in both the eyes of God and man. The 1$^{st}$ century sage Rabbi Chanina Ben Dosa teaches that the way others relate to us—if they like us or not—is an indication of how God relates to us:

> If the spirit of man is pleased with him [the leader], the spirit of God is pleased with him; but if the spirit of man is not pleased with him, the spirit of God is not pleased with him.[1]

Authority imposed upon people is power, not leadership, since to lead implies consent and approval. But the quality of being likable very often is misinterpreted in practice to mean that one should curry favor with others in order to receive their approval and support. As a result, political office-seekers routinely betray their purported ideals simply to garner votes.

A true leader on the other hand draws his strength and genuine connection to others from a sense of empathy. The Torah

33

relates[2] that God chose Joshua to succeed Moses because Joshua possessed a special spiritual quality—the ability to identify with everyone and to relate in love to each individual's inner character.[3] The ability to empathize with others, when developed and applied to interpersonal relations, manifests itself in the art of compromise. Compromise, in this sense, does not mean settling for second best or satisfying two opposite sides halfway; rather, it is nothing less than the art of unifying opposites for the sole purpose of achieving peace.

The test of a real leader, or any individual for that matter, is to know how to steadfastly guard moral and ethical principles while still maintaining the flexibility to facilitate compromise and conciliation.[4]

To understand this balance we need to delve into opposing opinions in Kabbalah regarding the dynamics involved in the creation of the world. In the 1500s, the Ari elucidated the concept of *tzimtzum*, the primordial "contraction" of God's infinite light, which made possible the creation of a "vacuum"—the mystical space wherein finite worlds could exist. Later Kabbalists argued whether the Ari's teachings were to be understood literally or figuratively. Did God literally and completely remove His Presence so an existence "outside" of Himself could come into being? Or, is the concept of *tzimtzum* to be taken figuratively and God's so-called absence is only a perception from a finite viewpoint?

(Hassidic philosophy is based on the understanding of *tzimtzum* as figurative—the impression of God's infinite light remains present in the apparent "vacuum," although His very essence is totally hidden; by aligning ourselves with the will of God, we can touch and reveal His infinite light, and ultimately, His very essence.)

The two understandings of *tzimtzum* give rise to two completely different ways of relating to reality, including the issue of compromise.

If the *tzimtzum* is to be understood literally, binary logic applies—God is either present or not, and one side of a disagreement is deemed right, and by implication, the other side wrong.[5] If, on the other hand, we understand *tzimtzum* as a phenomenon of our limited perception, there then is room for paradox and simultaneous contradictory realities—there is room for making judgments based on strict application of principles and for a simultaneous flexibility to facilitate compromise.

In Kabbalah, one of the deepest idioms employed to describe God's essence is "[the One] who sustains opposites." This idea—that plurality can be upheld and paradox resolved in the absolute oneness and unity of God—is the source of the consciousness that gives rise to compromise.

It is precisely in our world of apparent contradictions, where the Divine essence is hidden, that God wants us to reveal a higher logic whereby paradoxical and contradictory realities can coexist and ultimately be united. For this reason the sages ruled that it is better to pursue compromise whenever possible, thus allowing the kernel of truth on both sides to be revealed. Finding a mutually agreed-upon resolution is considered preferable to a mentality that conceives of *tzimtzum* literally, wherein one party to a conflict is absolutely right or wrong.

The two perceptions of *tzimtzum* and reality are symbolized by the two trees in the Garden of Eden. The Tree of Knowledge of Good and Evil, comprising two opposites, corresponds to binary logic. The Tree of Life, singular and unified by nature, corresponds to the ability to transcend a reality of mutual exclusion.

(Another symbol of a figurative rather than literal perception of *tzimtzum* is the Star of David, which consists of two oppositely oriented yet interlinked triangles, representing the intuitive ability of the Jewish mind to overcome the paradox of logical contradiction. Rather than viewing each triangle as a separate entity, the Star of David unites them.)

Cultivating a sense of compromise entails merging with the very heart of the Torah, which is "the Tree of Life for all those who grasp it," as taught in the Book of Proverbs. "Its ways are ways of pleasantness and all its pathways are peace."[6]

Standing on the periphery leads to a mentality of severe judgment, whereas the closer one approaches the heart of Torah the more one experiences God's oneness and His desire that we do all in our power to promote unity and peace in His world.[7]

## THE LIMITS OF COMPROMISE

What has been discussed up to this point regarding compromise does not apply if the conflict is between Torah and a superficial, materialistic view of reality. To think peace can be achieved by violating Torah is in fact the negation of peace, because, as stated above, the heart and soul of the Torah is genuine, lasting peace and compromise. It is therefore self-defeating to compromise Torah to conform to a reality that is based on a consciousness of duality.[8]

The desire to want to make Torah conform to the world originates in a fear of what Torah really is. This can be compared to an unmarried person who has a psychological fear of marriage, even though in truth he longs to marry. This causes a schizophrenic love-fear of the opposite sex.

The fear of true exposure to Torah in those who are unaware of its eternal relevance causes avoidance by some individuals, who, in their hearts, long for authentic, eternal values by which to live. The end result is the same love-fear response— the love of principles that emanate from Torah, yet fear of commitment to live by those principles. That fear may translate itself into an attitude that Torah is unrealistic and must, therefore, conform to prevailing man-made morality and ethics.

An example of this distorted perception of reality is how many people view Shabbat observance. At first, they balk at the number of actions forbidden, and view Shabbat as a day of severe restriction. But if they come to understand that these prohibitions create an atmosphere of welcome relief from the non-stop frantic haste of contemporary society, and a unique opportunity to cultivate an inner spiritual essence while strengthening family and community bonds, then they experience observance of the day quite differently. In a world screaming out for peace of mind, sense of purpose and spiritual contentment, Shabbat represents the ultimate gift of God's loving-kindness.

The fact that Shabbat is so misunderstood indicates just what an intense level of "sweetening" reality actually needs. It is therefore significant that the Messianic era is referred to as "a time that is entirely Shabbat,"[9] for then, the outer and inner perceptions of reality will be united.

Two examples from the physical world serve as parables for the paradoxical nature of reality as we experience it. When the human eye views an image, the image is projected onto the retina upside down. Only when the brain takes the image and reverses it do we see right side up. Another example: From where we stand on the planet, the sun's rising in the east and setting in the west clearly indicates that the sun revolves around the earth, yet from the perspective of the astronomer, the earth clearly revolves around the sun. The fact that God has created the world in a manner that both realities can be perceived as correct verifies the fact that the type of paradoxical logic we have been speaking of underlies all reality.

As a way to recognize and reconcile the paradoxes of nature, Rabbi Shalom Dovber of Lubavitch[10] would often recite the verse from Psalms, "Blessed are You God, teach me Your statutes."[11] Basing his interpretation on the double meaning of the Hebrew word for "statute" (*chok*), which also can be read as "engraving," he taught that "the statutes of Torah are engraved in every phenomenon of nature." His prayer was that God would teach him to appreciate that nature itself is a reflection of Torah and deepen his Torah study through which the revelation of Godliness is ever increased in the natural world.

The inverse is also true. By deepening our study of the natural world, we increase our understanding of both God and Torah. (This idea will be elaborated upon in the discussion of the fourth dynamic of leadership.)

The attitudes and beliefs emanating from different perceptions of the role of nature defined the essential battle over the soul of the Jewish people between the Greeks and the Jews at the time of Hanukah. On one side was the Greek system of binary logic, based on a superficial experience of nature, and on the other side the Jewish embrace of ultimate unity emanating from a Torah worldview.

The attitude of the Greeks had a genesis in their ancestry. Descended from Japheth, the son of Noah whose name literally means "beauty," the Greeks were meant to bring the beauty of the natural world into the study halls of Torah, in accordance with the blessing of Noah to his sons that "the beauty of Japheth will dwell in the tents of Shem."[12] (Shem was the brother of Japheth from whom the Semites, and particularly the Jewish people, descend.) However, this type of integration—which would have required compromise—was foreign to the Greeks and the system of binary logic by which they lived.

The art of compromise is what made the Jews different. The giving of the Torah at Sinai permeated Jewish consciousness with this ability, as we learn from two seemingly contradictory teachings.

The Midrash relates allegorically that before giving the Torah to the Jewish people, God "held the mountain over their head" and declared, "If you accept the Torah today, good; if not, this will be your burial place."[13] The implication here is that the Jews had no choice in the matter—they could accept the teachings and commandments of the Torah or die. However, the Torah itself, contradicts that notion:

> He [Moses] then took the Book of the Covenant,
> and read it in the ears of the people. They said,
> "All that God has spoken, we will do and we will
> hear."[14]

This statement expresses the epitome of free choice, not coercion as implied above, so which is true?

Both are true; indeed they represent one of the most primary of all paradoxes—that of free will and God's omnipotent and universal Providence. Each facet is absolutely true despite the fact that they appear to be mutually exclusive. The great 11th century philosopher, Maimonides,[15] states that even if all the seas were ink it would not be enough to write on this one issue. But complex as the idea may be, the wisdom to grasp the fact that both free will and God's Providence exist simultaneously, and that one does not negate the other, lies at the heart of one's ability to promote compromise and reconciliation.

In Kabbalah, the Midrash is explained by noting that the word "mountain" symbolizes light. Indeed, there are five two-syllable synonyms for "light" in Biblical Hebrew, each one ending with the syllable *har*, meaning "mountain": *zohar, bohar, tohar, nohar, tzohar*. (It is further noted in Kabbalah that the *tzimtzum* resulted in the disappearance of five levels of Divine light, corresponding to these five synonyms for "light.") Therefore, "mountain over their heads" represents an all-encompassing consciousness of God's light and love, and an awareness of the power of compromise that sustains opposites.

This analogy can be compared to a loving doctor who seemingly "coerces" his patient to undergo a certain treatment in order to heal him.[16] By holding the mountain—or His light—over their heads at Sinai, God "forced" the Jews to respond with great love from below to His overwhelming love from above.

According to tradition, it was not until the time of the Babylonian exile—nearly a thousand years later—that the Jewish people accepted the Torah completely out of free will.[17] It took generations to internalize and integrate Torah to the necessary extent. We might compare this process to what happens when a parent first forces a child to accept certain restrictions, such as not touching fire or not running into the street without looking; only later, as the child matures, does he or she accept the logic of those rules.

In the Messianic era, both "force" and acceptance will be manifest, but will occur nearly simultaneously and be suffused with pleasantness.

## COMPROMISING TORAH

We have spoken above about the importance of not compromising the principles of the Torah in order to adjust to perceived reality. But every general rule has an exception and this holds true here as well.[18]

Rabbi Shimon ben Lakish, a 3rd century sage who figures prominently in the Talmud, stated that sometimes compromising Torah "is its very foundation."[19]

Indeed, the Torah itself allows for nullification of almost all of its commandments when that is what is necessary to save a life, even in cases where only a suspicion exists that a life may be in danger. (The exceptions to this exception are three categories of commandments—prohibitions against murder, idolatry and sexual offenses, such as incest for example—that cannot be violated under any circumstances; indeed, many Jews have gone to their death rather than commit such heinous acts.)

Since every event we encounter—whether it be personal, communal, or global—is a manifestation of Divine Providence, being in a situation where we would be required, for example, to temporarily nullify the Torah laws of Shabbat in order to save a life, indicates that until then, on some conscious or unconscious level, our personal Shabbat was somehow not totally rectified. The temporary nullification is necessary in order to reach a newer and more elevated level of Shabbat. This is a particular example of the general principle of "descending for the ultimate sake of ascending." The descent actually creates a new and stronger foundation for future ascent.

Simply put, we need not despair when it is necessary to take one step back, if the end result is that we can then take two steps forward. In this way, all of life's negative moments become springboards for subsequent betterment. An awareness of this basic dynamic helps turn a negative or pessimistic attitude into a positive and optimistic view of life.

Ideally, human nature should be balanced enough to integrate all the wisdom of the Torah, but this is not always possible. The cosmic allegory of the "breaking of the vessels" (which we discussed in the previous chapter), when translated into psychological terms, serves as a powerful model to explain many common personal situations. People who take upon themselves more than they can handle, who push themselves too hard or stretch the cord of their minds and senses too strongly, may come to a situation where too much "light" or energy "breaks their vessels," that is, breaks the bounds of their realistic ability to integrate Torah wisdom into everyday life. This presents a potentially unhealthy psychological situation. In such a case, what may appear as a temporary compromise with regard to intense Torah-study for the ultimate sake of strengthening boundaries is, in fact, a positive development. This phenomenon is especially relevant to some newly-observant Jews, who in their initial excitement at finding the truth of Torah, dive headfirst into its sea of wisdom until almost drowning if not careful.[20]

Thus, the Ba'al Shem Tov spoke positively of taking a step backwards to regain a more holistic perspective, for example allowing time for relaxation and recreation as a means of fine-tuning a person's inner spiritual metabolism to delve into greater depths of wisdom. The state of temporary relaxation should produce a new injection of energy and renewed desire to learn.

A delicate balance is needed to properly integrate Torah on the personal psychological level as well on the community level. This is why every personality—as well as the personality of the community—is comprised of three components. We each embody within us the holy, the wicked, and the in-between.[21]

On occasion, due to immediate circumstances, one component of the personality, in its momentary enthusiasm, attempts to force a new reality on the whole personality. If an inner majority of one's being can live with it, the minority can be persuaded to accept the new situation and nullify or suppress itself for the good of the whole. Other times though, it happens that the inner majority is weak or apt to crumple under pressure. As a result, the suppressed psyche may rebel, requiring a total reassessment of the situation.

The human personality, as we know from both Jewish and modern psychological sources, is made up of multiple levels of consciousness and is incredibly complex. An individual must appoint an inner leader who can unite all the various powers of the soul, directing in unison thought, emotion and action. Without an inner leader, the human psyche can be compared to a rickety boat trying to traverse a raging river, ever in danger of capsizing.

The Hebrew letters of the name *Israel* may be permuted to read *li rosh*, meaning "I have a head," alluding to the natural internal leader of the Jew. Although the intellect must, at all times, be in contact with, and inspired by, the emotional and innate powers of the soul, the "head" must, nevertheless, assume its natural position as leader. This applies as well to how a community and its leaders should direct its affairs in the spirit of balance and compromise.

# EGO VS. SOUL

In order to cultivate an inner sense of compromise, one needs a balanced ego. An inflated sense of self that dominates thought, speech, and action, creates an "I vs. you" mentality of binary logic that makes compromise impossible. When the ego is refined and the self seeks to reunite with its source in God, the end result is the ability to see a bigger picture of reality—the Divine outlook on life.[22]

In true paradoxical form, ideal leadership emanates not from the powerfully inflated ego that is commonly evidenced by persons who hold the reigns of power in our world, but rather from genuine humility that carries within it an inner strength to empower and inspire others.[23] Indeed, when properly cultivated, humility creates a rectified ego able to deal responsibly with the temptations and the peripheral trappings of power, leadership, and public exposure.

While it is taken for granted that the average person has to continually struggle with ego refinement, it is assumed that those who have reached higher spiritual planes have, in so doing, also achieved a higher level of self-awareness. True as this may be, it does not automatically follow that such people are exempt from the ongoing work of ego refinement. In the Talmud, the sages go so far as to state:

> The greater the person, the greater his evil inclination.[24]

This implies that such people, because of their advanced level, must confront even greater, though more subtle, challenges and further continue the work of ego refinement in order to reach even higher levels of consciousness.[25]

Although many techniques have been developed to assist one in the arduous task of ego rectification, there are no set formulas that will work for everyone. It is, therefore, important to find a spiritual leader with whom one can identify and feel a deep soul-connection. A true leader, along with guiding and inspiring, helps one to contact the place deep within the soul where ego clarification can occur. In this sense, marital partners, parents, siblings, and friends can all assume the role of guide and leader for each other at different stages in life.

The process of ego rectification may proceed in an orderly, disciplined manner, or at times may be quite sudden and powerful, coming as a total shock. The Midrash relates that the Israelites were so awe-struck by their initial encounter with God at Mt. Sinai that their souls repeatedly left their bodies in order to cleave to the Divine Presence and that they had to be brought back to life time after time.[26]

The image of the soul departing and returning in response to the words of God alludes to one of the fundamental dynamics of the soul, referred to in Kabbalah as "running and returning." The source of this concept is Ezekiel's vision of the chariot, the same vision in which the mystery word *chashmal* appears. In the center of this electrifying energy, Ezekiel saw "living creatures" whom he described as having the figures of human beings, but each with four faces (that of a man, a lion, an ox, and an eagle) and each with four wings:

> And the living creatures ran and returned like
> the appearance of a flash of lightning.[27]

It is explained in the Talmud[28] that Ezekiel is describing here the "pulsation" of certain angels who ascend higher and higher toward Divine Presence, and upon reaching the apex of their "run" attain a glimpse of the Divine light. The shock of the encounter, however, causes them to retreat immediately and "return" below. Nonetheless, their desire to experience Divine revelation motivates them to ascend again. This process of run and return in the celestial worlds continues endlessly.

Similarly, the soul longs to ascend and reunite with its Divine source, but is ever drawn back to the body through which it must attempt to fulfill its mission on earth.

The basic bodily rhythm of the heart beating manifests this spiritual reality within the most essential pulse of life. The dualistic nature of humanity, and in fact all of reality, being simultaneously spiritual and material, mirrors this dynamic as well. This apparent dualism may lead to an initial illusion of binary logic, which on a superficial level is true, but which disappears when viewed within a higher spiritual dimension. We are constantly bidden to transcend the lower awareness of reality in order ultimately to unify all opposites.

It is taught in Hassidism that one of the most effective ways to begin the process of soul purification is not necessarily by intense, inner spiritual work, but by doing good for others. Sometimes we are so absorbed in our own selves, even if for positive reasons, that we lose sight of the broader reality around us. But if we take care to pay attention to, and to be grateful for, the continual goodness shown to us by God, we also become motivated to emulate His goodness by doing good for others.[29]

Hillel, the great sage of the 1st century BCE, taught, "Be like the students of Aaron—loving peace and pursuing peace; loving all people and drawing them close to Torah."[30]

Hillel used Aaron, the first High Priest, as his model because Aaron was especially beloved by the people due to his continual efforts to promote compromise, reconciliation, and peace. If two people—a married couple or a pair of friends, for example—were experiencing difficulties, Aaron would go to each party individually and, by stretching the truth, would make assurances that the other one had expressed words of love and wanted to resolve their dispute. In this way he facilitated peace. The example set by Aaron was firmly established by the later sages when they stated: "For the sake of peace one is allowed to change [the truth]."[31] Note that the precise language is not "to lie" but "to change." According to the lower logic it may, in fact, be lying, but from a higher perspective it is adjusting logic in order to embrace both sides of a dispute for the ultimate purpose of compromise and peace.

An example of this is found in a dispute between Hillel, and another great sage of his time, Shamai, as to whether it is permissible to describe a bride as beautiful, if, in fact, she is not. Hillel taught that all brides are beautiful, and so did the other sages concur.[32]

# THE TWO SIDES OF JUSTICE

One of the most pivotal Torah admonitions, which appears in conjunction with the commandments to establish a court system is, "Justice, justice shall you pursue."[33] A natural question, asked by commentators, is why the word "justice" is repeated. In light of all that has been discussed above regarding the sense of compromise, we can understand the repetition to signify that the Torah is urging anyone in the role of judge or mediator to seek out justice on both sides of a question. Ultimately, the common denominator uniting all parties in an argument is God Himself, Whose essential Oneness encompasses all points of view. Torah serves as His instrument to make peace and build a just society.

Making the most of Torah wisdom, King Solomon gained the respect of his people as an inspired judge. The most famous example of the cases he adjudicated was the dispute of the two women who both claimed the same baby as their own.[34]

The two women reported before the king that they had both given birth in the same inn within days of each other, but one of the babies had died due to the negligence of the mother who had suffocated him accidentally in her sleep. Now the accusation was being made that this mother subsequently switched her own dead baby with the other woman's live child. Nothing identified the infant as to which woman he truly belonged.

As the two women argued before the king, each swearing the child was hers, Solomon called for a sword to be brought to him. "Cut the living child in two," he ordered, "and give half to one and half to the other."

In response to the king's order, one woman began to plead, "Please, my lord, give her the living infant, and do not put it to death!" But the other woman defiantly declared, "Neither mine nor yours shall he be. Cut!"

By threatening to cut the baby in half,[35] King Solomon "shocked" the true mother into expressing her love, compassion, and selflessness, thus clarifying the truth. Only the real mother would love her baby so much that she could selflessly give him up in order to save him.

King Solomon then pronounced his judgment: "Give her the living newborn and do not put it to death; she is his mother."

This, of course, is not an example of compromise. Although the sages preferred compromise whenever possible, it does not mean that strict judgment is somehow negative or never to be employed. It would be the epitome of binary logic to actually pit strict judgment versus compromise.

The Torah is called both a "Torah of truth" and a "Torah of loving-kindness."[36] Judgment and compassion[37] are two necessary aspects of God's unity manifest in our world. Every individual spends a lifetime learning to balance and harmonize these two aspects, until true inner peace is created. Torah comes to assist this process by establishing the basic framework of human conduct and interaction based on God's wisdom and love of His creation.

The opportunity to exercise judgment and facilitate compromise is available to every person in a host of situations on a daily basis. The choice is ever present to judge others favorably, always looking to emulate both Aaron by pursuing and creating peace and Joshua by establishing a personal rapport with all people.

The teaching of the sages that each individual is as important as a whole world[38] not only develops self-esteem, but also underscores the value of each human being and the awesome responsibility we bear in rectifying "our" world. Leadership is not the exclusive realm of the elite or powerful, but rather is a virtue to be developed and expressed by everyone in all facets of life. Every person has the chance to assume a position of leadership no matter how small the circle of influence. As stated earlier, the Ultimate Leader will be revealed when enough individuals develop their leadership potential.

The Ultimate Leader—as part of his leadership role—will be first and foremost a teacher and a judge. By establishing a soul-connection with all the people, he will lay a foundation of judgment based on peace and compromise.

As the Messianic era quickly approaches and as the world continues to change at breathtaking speed, it becomes increasingly important to pursue the inner spiritual work needed to reveal the truth of Torah and the peace that is its essence.

To save a life is to save a world, and to bring the Ultimate Leader even one step closer to fulfilling his mission is ultimately to redeem the entire world.

# 3

# Second Dynamic

## THE DRIVE FOR WHOLENESS

The inner motivation of the first dynamic of leadership, the art of compromise, is a sincere desire for peace, and the secret of peace is wholeness.

Peace and wholeness are inextricably linked. The Hebrew word for "peace" (*shalom*) derives from the word for "perfect, whole, complete" (*shalem*). This, then, is the second dynamic of leadership—a belief in an ultimate utopian state of peace, perfection, and wholeness, which though not fully achievable in the present, is nevertheless a goal to which one should aspire. It is precisely because perfection always seems to be just beyond reach that a true leader must stretch his every faculty to be "ahead of his time." By so doing, he draws the future into the present, bringing a state of transcendence into normative reality.

When a leader manifests this state of transcendence he appears, at least to an outsider, to be leading in a supernatural or miraculous manner. But to those close to him, the supernatural seems perfectly natural; they become so accustomed to the extraordinary qualities he embodies that, after a while, they take the miraculous almost for granted, because it has become part of their world order. Thus the aura of leadership is created not by just theorizing about rectifying reality, but by actually creating the atmosphere and circumstances in which people can experience wholeness and inner peace in the present.

This is not to suggest that a leader depends on miracles; indeed he does not.[1] Rather, by living just beyond his capabilities, he cultivates his deepest reservoirs of potential, transmuting the supernatural into the natural.

In Hassidic thought this is referred to as living on a plane "one handbreath above ground." Rabbi Shmuel of Lubavitch[2] taught that when confronted with an obstacle, one should simply jump over it, because in so doing, one will nullify its existence. Whereas every obstacle in our finite world has a limit, the soul has none—it always has the potential to draw upon its unlimited, infinite, eternal source.

Two of the best Biblical examples of those who leapt over obstacles are Mordechai and Esther—the hero and heroine of Purim whose story is told in the Book of Esther.

In the days following the Babylonian exile, when the Jews chafed under the domination of the Persians, Mordechai stubbornly refused to bow to Haman, the king's chief minister, seeing this act as a violation of the Torah's prohibition against bowing down to any power other than God.

Enraged, by what he perceived as one Jew's arrogance, Haman devised a plot to exterminate all the Jews within the empire.

A decree went out, signed by the king, ordering a wholesale massacre of the Jews on the 13th day of the month of *Adar*. Despite what must have seemed as insurmountable odds, Mordechai did not plunge into despair. Rather, he instructed his ward, Esther—who some years before had been inducted into the king's harem and who now was queen—to petition the king to overturn the decree.

The risks for Esther were enormous. She would have to approach the king unbidden, an offense punishable by death; and, if she survived, then she would have to reveal her secret Jewish identity. Struck by the magnitude of the obstacles before her, Esther hesitated. But Mordechai spurred her on, matter-of-factly declaring:

> "If you persist in keeping silent at a time like this, relief and deliverance will come to the Jews from another place, while you and your father's house will perish. And who knows whether it was just for such a time as this that you attained the royal position."[3]

Totally convinced by Mordechai's argument, Esther agreed to risk her life and try to save her people. She told Mordechai:

> "Go, assemble all the Jews to be found in Shushan, and fast for me. Do not eat or drink for three days, night or day. I, with my maids, will fast also. Then I will go to the King though it is unlawful. And if I perish, I perish."[4]

Esther won, of course. The Jews were saved. Through determined effort, Esther and Mordechai overcame all obstacles and turned the tables so completely that Haman was hanged on the very gallows he had constructed for Mordechai.

The fact that God's Name is never mentioned in the entire Book of Esther represents the miraculous manifesting itself in the historical process incognito, so much so that it appears totally natural.

Another important example of one who managed to transcend all earthly obstacles was King David, the exemplary leader who is perhaps the most beloved of all figures in the Bible precisely because he was so human. God graced him with a supernatural quality that allowed him to rise above all obstacles and defeat all foes. (The most famous of his victories is, of course, that over Goliath.)

It was King David who established Jerusalem as Israel's eternal capital and paved the way for the eventual building of the Temple, the place where spiritual and material, infinite and temporal, unite. It is recorded[5] that ten continual miracles occurred while the First Temple, built by King David's son, King Solomon, was standing. Inasmuch as the miracles were ongoing, they appeared to be part of the natural order.

The desire of the soul to transcend the limits of the natural order and strive for perfected reality—to "run and return" as discussed in the previous chapter—translates into attempts to manifest the infinite light of God within the finite reality of our world, in the here and now. We do not "run"—allowing the soul to fly upwards towards its source—in order to feel good or indulge the senses; we do so in order to glimpse a vision of perfection which then must be integrated into everyday life until it becomes our true nature—and that is the meaning of "return."

The greater the obstacle, the higher we have to leap. Reaching beyond our apparent dualistic world of binary logic allows us to unify opposites, thus creating oneness and peace. At this elevated level we become aware that the essence of the spiritual longs to merge with the physical. When this union occurs, the result is—if even for a moment—the experience of peace, completeness, and perfection. Such precious, rare moments serve as the driving force in the soul to expand what is at first a fleeting experience and make it last longer and longer until it encompasses more and more of our reality.[6]

As difficult as this may be to believe, we know from history that such an experience was readily achievable in ages past. The Jewish tradition, from its inception to the present, brims with examples of men and women who could prophesy about the future and perform miracles. In the time of the First Temple there were "schools of prophecy," where students were taught the Jewish tradition of expanded Divine consciousness. These teachings prepared the students to experience life in a holistic, unified manner, and to orient the soul to seek its own perfection in God's oneness. The Talmud states that, while only forty-eight male and seven female prophets are specifically mentioned in the Bible due to the eternal nature of their message, there were in fact over a million prophets in Jewish history.[7]

As a general rule though, these people did not undertake to reveal the supernatural for their own sake or for the thrill of the altered-consciousness experience. Rather, the miracles they performed resulted from a direct command and experience of God, or as a solution to an extreme situation. For the prophet and miracle worker, the individual prophecy or miracle was not intended to be a one-time aberration, but a glimpse into a higher dimension of a perfected reality that could be revealed and experienced by everyone.[8] When some people were distressed that others were prophesying in the Israelite camp, Moses countered by expressing the wish, "Would it be that all the people of God were prophets!"[9]

In the Messianic era, when what we now consider miraculous will indeed be natural, we will reach such an elevated consciousness of perfect completeness that the wish of Moses will be fulfilled.

## INDIVISIBILITY OF ONENESS

The achievement of wholeness and completeness depends on the total dedication of the soul to the extent that one is willing to give up one's life for a holy cause.[10] In so doing, one reveals the highest level of the soul—the level referred to in Kabbalah as *yechidah*, "the single one" or "the unique one"—which transcends the confines of material plurality and separateness. At this level, the ultimate oneness and wholeness of God can be seen reflected in every aspect of reality.

Toward the end of bringing his people to this level of dedication and awareness, a leader inspires a group of diverse individuals to dedicate their lives and energies to one holy cause, thus molding them into a single entity which reveals the collective unity of *yechidah*.

An entity whose essence is wholeness is by definition indivisible. The Ba'al Shem Tov taught: "if you take hold of a part of an essence, you take hold of its entirety."[11] Every moment of time, in potential, contains all of time; every point of space, in potential, contains all of space. Conversely though, if you take a part away from something that is by essence whole, you have blemished its perfection. This apparent paradox can only be resolved through total dedication of the soul.

We are taught in Kabbalah that there are three entities—
each Divine in its source though existing on the physical plane—
whose essence is defined by wholeness:

- the Torah

- the Jewish people

- the land of Israel

If a Torah scroll lacks one letter or even part of a letter, the
whole scroll is invalid until corrected. The six-hundred-thousand
who went out of Egypt represent the totality of all primordial
Jewish souls.[12] These souls correspond to the six-hundred-
thousand letters of the Torah. Similar to a Torah scroll, which is
invalidated by a blemish in even one letter, so are the Jewish
people considered incomplete if even one soul is in pain or has
strayed from his Jewish tradition. Therefore "all of Israel are
responsible one for another."

This is graphically illustrated by the story of the Jewish
people's initial entry into the Promised Land.[13] As the Book of
Joshua relates,[14] when they reached the walls of Jericho—a heavily
fortified city considered the gateway to the Promised Land—they
circled it seven times and blew the shofar, only to see the walls fall
down before their eyes. Commanded by God to complete the
conquest, they were nevertheless forbidden to take any booty or
any object belonging to the inhabitants as all was to be dedicated
to God.

The Jews scrupulously followed this dictate, except for one
person, Achan, who stole certain valuables.

Not realizing that something had gone terribly wrong, they
moved on to the next city to be conquered, the city of Ai, and
there met a tragic defeat with many of their number killed.
Traumatized by the experience, they pleaded to know why God

had abandoned them and in response God told them that the defeat was the result of one of their own having betrayed the integrity of the whole. [15]

The entirety of the Jewish people and their fate as a whole is here seen to be encapsulated in the persona and deeds of each individual Jew—as noted above, "if you take hold of a part of an essence, you take hold of its entirety."

Like the Jewish people, the land of Israel is whole and the separation of even one part betrays, on some level, the totality of the rest. For this reason, all Messianic prophecies revolve around the Jewish people returning and redeeming the entire land of Israel. For only when all the Jewish people return to the complete Jewish homeland will Isaiah's prophecy be fulfilled. Then the oneness of God, the source of all wholeness, will be obvious to the whole world, as Isaiah proclaims:

> For from Zion shall come forth Torah, the word of God from Jerusalem. He [God] will judge among the nations and arbitrate for the many peoples. And they shall beat their swords into plowshares, and their spears into pruning hooks; nation shall not lift up sword against nation, neither shall they learn war anymore. [16]

# A CARING HEART

It is taught in Hassidism that "there is nothing as whole as a broken heart." [17] A broken heart is "whole" for it is the soul's prerequisite state for conceiving wholeness. Only a broken heart is capable of identifying and empathizing with all that is presently broken in the world and motivating a person to rectify it. This degree of sensitivity, though, if not handled correctly, blinds one to the issues at hand and engulfs the soul in an emotional whirlpool. A perfect balance of caring and independent fortitude must be forged. No heart must be bigger, nor shoulders broader, than the individual who accepts the burden of leadership.

Too often, however, modern models of leadership err in the opposite direction—they appear as cold, calculating individuals, whose concern for those they represent is secondary to their own interest and struggle for political survival. Contemporary society has a strange fascination with those ruthless enough to rise to power and fame through any means necessary. But a true leader is defined by his compassionate caring for others, rather than by detachment. Far from being insular, or above emotional attachment to his constituency, he works tirelessly for the sake of his community, leaving no stone unturned in his quest to assist others.

Compassion involves empathy of the most intimate nature, and the one who wishes to lead must have the utmost sensitivity to others' pain, as it is written: "For the compassionate one will lead them."[18]

Every person has daily opportunities to show compassion and understanding, and in so doing reveal his or her innate leadership qualities. Even small gestures of caring should not be underestimated—for the recipient as well as the giver.[19]

The best model of compassion in history—long before he became a leader, when he was just a simple shepherd—is none other than Moses. The Midrash[20] relates that God saw his innate leadership qualities in his tender care of the lambs in his charge.

One day, as Moses was tending the flock of his father-in-law Jethro, a lamb scampered off, and Moses followed it. The little lamb kept running until it came upon a pool of water and there it stopped to drink. When Moses caught up with it, he said, "I did not know that you ran away because you were thirsty. I am so sorry that all this running has made you tired." And he hoisted the lamb on his shoulder and carried it back to the herd. The Midrash concludes:

> The Holy One then said: "Because you showed
> such compassion in tending the flock of a
> mortal, I vow that you shall become shepherd of
> Israel, the flock that is Mine."

Moses was the leader who took the Jewish people out of Egypt and who brought them to Mt. Sinai where they received the Torah. Perhaps more than any one else, Moses understood the statement of the sages, "The secrets of the Torah are only given over to one who is worried in his heart."[21]

The worry referred to here is not from a lack of trust or sense of security, nor is it caused by the transitory matters of this world; rather, it is a deep, existential uneasiness with our present imperfect reality. It is the worry that causes us to search and yearn for perfection and wholeness. True, we are taught to accept that "all is for the good" and that God is perfect, implying that all is exactly as it should be. On the other hand, it is clear that due to man's free will, the world situation—at least from a superficial view—is less a reflection of God's perfection than of man's accumulated imperfections. More than just accepting the world as it is, we are commanded in the Torah and implored by the sages and prophets to become partners with God in rectifying and elevating the world.

The sincere probing of the heart and mind, and the worry and anxiety it causes, creates a vessel to receive the secrets of life and Torah in order to sweeten reality. Torah gives direction and meaning to life, and though it does not guarantee ease and comfort, it does insure that life's inevitable struggles and trials are for a constructive purpose. The secrets of the Torah, when deeply integrated, help alleviate and sweeten the suffering all around us.

If the suffering of so many leaves no effect on the heart and mind, there is no motivation to try to effect change. The incentive to perfect the world comes from a worried heart and the empathy one feels to all who fall victim to life's seeming imperfections.

Conversely, King Solomon teaches, "When there is worry in a man's heart, he should suppress it, and let a good word convert it to gladness."[22]

If the worry of the heart is not put into perspective it can lead to deep depression and inaction. The sages have suggested a number of ways to overcome dejection of the heart,[23] including:

- reflection to find the aspect of the personality that requires rectification and is causing the worry

- rejecting worrisome thoughts by dwelling on positive thoughts

- confiding one's worries to a friend

The end of the verse "let a good word convert it to gladness" illustrates how speech leads the way, in this case, by restoring a measure of peace of mind. It further shows how we can serve as interim leaders to friends and family through a simple word of encouragement or empathy.

While everyone would want, if possible, a life free from petty worries, the deep-seated anxiety of a true leader is rooted in the inexplicable paradoxes of existence. Rather than being dejected by them, he uses all of his strength to bring sweetening and rectification wherever possible.[24]

# BODY AND SOUL

Although the foundation of wholeness lies in the unity of spiritual and physical, the fact remains that when we experience the world, we face the apparent dichotomy between the spiritual and the physical. Perhaps the clearest example of this dichotomy is the relationship between the soul and the body. The ongoing struggle between the forces of soul and body—and their concurrent partnership—can be called the classic example of a love-hate relationship. Yet, if the basic drive in the soul for wholeness is to become a living reality, the apparent opposites of spiritual and physical must be united.

Wholeness is beyond our grasp if the mind is caught in the clutches of a logic based on the mutual exclusivity of the spiritual and physical. The Torah—and ancient as well as contemporary sages—teaches that it is the mission of each individual Jew to uplift and rectify the physical world by transfusing material reality with spiritual energy. A Jew is not uplifted by fleeing from the world to some spiritual ivory tower, or by submerging totally in the physical at the expense of the soul. Rather, a Jew achieves wholeness by elevating the spark of Divinity in all physical existence to its spiritual source.

This fundamental philosophy explains the reason for creation, the function of the human soul, as well as the purpose of the Torah and its commandments.

Jacob, the patriarch who achieved wholeness in his lifetime, blessed each of his twelve sons on his deathbed. His blessings to Zevulun and Issachar are interpreted by the sages to be blessings for physical wealth and Torah study, respectively. The tribe of Zevulun was known to be very generous in supporting the tribe of Issachar so they could pursue their studies, and as a result, Issachar produced many of the members of the Sanhedrin, the Jewish Supreme Court. The relationship between these two brothers has remained a model of cooperation throughout Jewish history. The fact that Zevulun, the merchant, received his blessing before Issachar, the scholar, is treated with great importance in the Kabbalah[25] which explains that pursuing business, on a certain level, represents "surrounding reality" and mastering the physical world.

After Adam ate from the Tree of Knowledge, the earth was cursed to bring forth weeds and thorns and man was forced to work hard "by the sweat of [his] brow" to bring forth bread from the earth.[26] The toil of earning one's livelihood is thus seen both as a "curse" and as an opportunity to fulfill man's basic function in the world.

The danger in this universal predicament is that, instead of the pursuit of business simply surrounding reality, it becomes *all* reality. Those who make this mistake end up going in circles, spending much of their lives unhappy in unfulfilling jobs. This, in turn, leads to incredible degrees of boredom and frustration as they watch their own meaningless lives passing before them.

The feeling of being completely disconnected from the source of one's livelihood is the ultimate manifestation of the "curse" of Adam. One of the greatest blessings in life is to love one's work, so much so, that it is considered an indispensable part of self-expression and fulfillment.

The term "life's work" describes a state of mind where there is no essential distinction between what you do for a living, what your beliefs are, and who you are as a person. This state of integrity represents the epitome of wholeness—in that through your life's work you have the satisfaction of fulfilling your soul's purpose in this world.

This brings us to another deep and surprising secret of the Kabbalah:[27] the ultimate source of the primordial cosmic vessels, which broke because they were unable to contain the Divine light, is even higher than the source of the light itself—the source of the physical is higher than the source of the spiritual.

This is further illustrated by an analogy used in Hassidic teachings: when a stone wall collapses, the highest of the stones fall the farthest from the base.

The Ari explained that the source of the vessels is the impression of God's Presence that remained in the vacuum resulting from the *tzimtzum* (the contraction of the Divine light that initially filled all reality). This impression[28] is the raw, "formless" material out of which the vessels were created. At a certain state in the development of the vessels, they were unable to hold the Divine light that shone into them and broke. The Ari taught that our mission in this world is to redeem the fallen sparks scattered throughout the world as a result of the primordial "breaking of the vessels."[29]

The Ari also taught that the protracted exile of the Jewish people from the land of Israel, though painful and seemingly endless, in truth is a necessary stage in the ultimate redemption of the world. Themselves scattered to the four corners of the earth, the Jewish people were destined to uplift the sparks trapped in the shells of the material world and bring them back to their source in Torah, to the collective Jewish soul, and to the land of Israel. For this reason, the ingathering of the exiles to Israel in our day is a sign of the quickly-approaching Messianic era.

The universal vision of unity, wholeness, and complete redemption of the world has driven the Jewish people and helped them to survive against all odds and historic precedents. It is this same vision that propels Jewish leaders in every generation as they attempt to instill these concepts in the hearts of their contemporaries. Though at times it may seem unreal, or even impossible, for the world to reach such an exalted level, nonetheless, by striving towards that end, we can to bring these ideals into our daily existence.

We learn this from the story of Abraham. The Torah states that when the father of monotheism was old, God blessed him in all things. This statement is somewhat cryptic:

> And Abraham was old, coming into days, and
> God blessed Abraham with all.[30]

Kabbalah explains that Abraham, through a lifetime of spiritual elevation, finally reached a level where he could transcend time—literally "coming into days." Not only did he experience the next world, but he could manifest it in this world as well.

For us, even dreaming of a utopian world, let alone acting upon our convictions, helps create it here and now.

Furthermore, the study of the inner dimensions of Torah "sweetens the judgments" of an unrectified world and arouses great Divine compassion. On a personal level, the study of the secrets of Torah in Kabbalah "purifies the air" of unrectified personality. For in truth, the study of Kabbalah demands the purification of every aspect of consciousness, and eventually the unconscious mind as well. (Attempting to learn the inner dimensions of Torah while ignoring the need to constantly refine the ego may not only be fruitless but destructive as well.)

After tasting the sweetness of Torah, our whole being longs for more, thus giving us incentive to purify our vessels for the ever-greater light waiting to be admitted. As our vessels become more purified, we begin to integrate the essential unity of creation as revealed by God, the Source of all perfection.

When the essential entities of wholeness—Torah, the Jewish people, and the land of Israel—are transformed from individual flames into a unified, fiery torch of love for God, then His compassion will be aroused to such an extent that the world will be flooded by the knowledge of God "as the waters cover the sea,"[31] to borrow the words of Isaiah.

Our longing to experience the oneness of God from below draws down a waterfall of love from above. The integration of fire and water is the essence of heaven, as reflected in the fact that the Hebrew word for "heaven" (*shamayim*) is a combination of the words for "fire" (*eish*) and "water" (*mayim*).

Heaven must be brought down to earth; spirituality must be integrated with physical reality. Every thought, speech, and action that unites both poles helps prepare the world for its ultimate redemption.

May we all actualize our individual sparks and become leaders in our own right, thereby fulfilling our mission in life to bring the Ultimate Leader and the Ultimate Redemption here and now.

# 4

# Third Dynamic

## THE POWER OF COMPASSION TO INSPIRE

Do not be scornful of any person and do not be disdainful of anything, for there is no person without his hour and nothing without its place.[1]

We may understand this statement of the sages to support our premise that every person has the potential for leadership; it just awaits the right time to manifest itself. That "hour" is the time when one's soul-root shines most strongly. And it is in the essence of the soul-root that the potential for leadership lies, according to Kabbalah.

Every leader awaits his "hour" at the level of the soul-root, in the deepest realms of the super-consciousness. This most-elevated aspect of the soul is called in Kabbalah "the unknowable head."[2] In fact, it is so unknowable, so hidden, that one is totally unaware of the extent of one's own potential, and of course so are others. Nonetheless, if the person dedicates himself intensely to serve God and emulate His Divine attributes,[3] some of this latent leadership potential will become evident.

At this point, a crucial transformation must occur if the leader's circle of influence is to grow. For a leader to make a mark on a community, he must be able to inspire those around him to reach ever-greater levels of connection with God and their fellow human beings.[4]

The ability to motivate others, though, ultimately rests upon his own inner level of inspiration. This, then, is the third dynamic of leadership—the evolution and development of inspiration, which is intrinsically bound to the attribute of compassion. (We have previously described how compassion is God's determining factor in identifying a potential leader.)

Viewing the world through compassionate eyes gives the potential leader the ability to see beyond superficiality and first impressions, allowing the inner spark within those he encounters to shine forth. He continues to nurture these newly revealed sparks of holiness in others and lead them in compassion. In the words of Isaiah:

> ...for he who shows them compassion will lead
> them, by fountains of water he will guide them.[5]

He who wishes to lead must overcome his desire to judge others, allowing a sense of compassion to form his basic worldview. First, he cultivates compassion and understanding for everyone, recognizing the descent of every soul from its exalted source on high to this lowly world—its "fall" into an individual state of exile; he looks beyond superficial appearances (the result of the fall) to the most inner potential of the soul. Next, he feels unlimited compassion for the people of Israel as a whole, as they continue their ancient struggle to progress from exile and oppression towards total redemption. Lastly, he relates personally to the exile of God's Presence, the *Shechinah*, and to God's pain, as it were, in bearing a world so in need of rectification and unification.[6]

Each of these levels of compassion elicits a response from above—a response that is felt as Divine inspiration within the heart of the person who experiences the compassion.[7]

From the verse in Deuteronomy[8]—"And God will give you compassion and have compassion upon you"—we learn that compassion, and inspiration in the ultimate sense, are gifts from God. As we become aware of the need to be more sensitive to others, God graces us with that ability. This creates a spiral effect in the soul, where compassion produces the inspiration to act, which, in turn, draws down additional compassion and inspiration from above.

Thus, the sense of inspiration is a fundamental motivating force in all human beings, driving us not merely to empathize with the pain of others, but to act directly and forcefully to alleviate that pain. Though inspiration is legitimately channeled into a wide range of creative endeavors, its primary purpose, especially in a leader, is to rectify reality and elevate all those around him, thus revealing God's redeeming presence in every situation of life.

## COMPASSION AND SELFLESSNESS

A tradition handed down by the sages teaches that the Ultimate Leader, the Messiah, will be the reincarnation of the soul of the model leader, Moses.[9]

Moses began his vocation as leader when his compassion was kindled at the sight of his fellow Jew being beaten by a cruel Egyptian. By saving the Jew and slaying the Egyptian, Moses, who at the time was a prince of Egypt, forever threw his lot in with his people. Years later, after he demonstrated such tender care of the flock belonging to his father-in-law Jethro (as described earlier), God appeared to him at the burning bush with the directive to return to Egypt and assume the leadership of the Jewish people. From that point on, Moses became the great defender of Israel, pleading its cause before God, even after the grievous sin of the golden calf.

Even greater than Moses' compassion upon the people was his selflessness. The Torah attests to this: "And the man Moses was exceedingly humble, more than any man on the face of the earth."[10] Twice, in response to complaints by the people, Moses in self-deprecating reference to himself and his brother Aaron exclaimed, "...and what are we?"[11]

> So Moses and Aaron said to all the Israelites, "By evening, you shall know it was God who brought you out from the land of Egypt; and in the morning, then you shall see the glory of God, because He has heard your murmurings against God. For what are we, that you murmur against us?" And Moses said, "This shall be, when God shall give you in the evening meat to eat, and in the morning bread to the full; for that God hears your murmurings which you murmur against Him; and what are we? Your murmurings are not against us, but against God."

In Kabbalah, the word for "what" (*mah*), refers to the second of the ten *sefirot*, the *sefirah* of *chochmah* ("wisdom"). When the letters of *chochmah* are permuted they spell *koach mah* meaning "the power of selflessness." The wisdom of Moses derived from his great humbleness, which allowed him to become the perfect "empty" vessel through which God's will could be manifest.

Although the Ultimate Leader (the reincarnation of Moses) will likewise possess a deep sense of selflessness, his most pronounced attribute will be his compassion for the Jewish people and the entire world. Whereas Moses is most strongly associated with the *sefirah* of *chochmah*, whose inner dimension is selflessness, the Ultimate Leader is most connected to the *sefirah* of *tiferet* ("beauty"), whose inner dimension is compassion.[12] With his power to inspire, the Ultimate Leader will bring out the inner brilliance of each person, creating a beautiful rainbow of unity of all souls and of all peoples.

The people of Israel are innately beautiful, as described in allegorical form throughout King Solomon's masterpiece, the Song of Songs. Poverty of spirit, a result of the long exile, tends to cover up this beauty until it is sometimes hidden beneath a superficial cover of external ugliness. Through a deep inner vision of the intrinsic beauty of the Jewish people, the Ultimate Leader will be able to reveal once again what is hidden.

The *sefirah* of *tiferet* is situated in the middle column of the ten *sefirot*, from where it balances and integrates the left and right sides with its inspirational motivating force of compassion. Compassion can be initiated and expressed in two ways—through prayer and through acts of mercy.

The "right side" in Kabbalah represents acts of loving-kindness that descend from giver to recipient, whereas the "left side" represents the uplifting of the soul in prayer to arouse Divine mercy and compassion.

The 2nd century sage, Rabbi Eliezer,[13] taught that one should first perform an act of compassion and only afterward turn to God in prayer to arouse His Divine compassion. Thus, every morning before praying, he would give a coin to a needy person. The Ba'al Shem Tov and his disciples encouraged their followers to adopt this practice, as well as to become involved throughout the day with the welfare of their communities and actively engage in acts of kindness. This, in turn, they taught, would make one's prayers for Divine compassion more potent and concrete.

The teaching of Rabbi Eliezer has its Biblical support in the order of events that occurred when Jacob met Rachel for the first time.[14]

The Torah relates that as Jacob neared the birthplace of his mother Rebbeca, where he had been sent by his parents to find a wife, he came upon a group of shepherds congregating by a well. They informed him that they were awaiting the arrival of other shepherds, for only with a joint effort could they roll away the heavy stone covering the well and water their sheep. At that very moment Rachel came by with her flock. Jacob was so inspired upon seeing his future wife that he single-handedly pushed away the stone from the well and then watered her sheep. Only afterwards did he approach her.

Rabbi Shneur Zalman of Liadi,[15] in his classic work, the *Tanya*, cites this story when examining the characteristic of compassion. He explains that Jacob, upon seeing Rachel for the first time, envisioned all future Jewish souls who would come from the twelve tribes of Israel—his twelve sons by Rachel, her sister Leah and their maidservants; this vision intuitively aroused in him tremendous compassion. Thus inspired, he was immediately moved to perform the kind act of lifting the heavy stone off the well and watering the animals. Only afterwards did he kiss her, raising his voice in prayer for all the souls of Israel who would be so in need of compassion in the future, as the Torah relates:

> And he watered the sheep of Laban, his mother's brother. And Jacob then kissed Rachel and cried [out in prayer].

The Hebrew words for "and he watered" (*vayashk*) and "and he kissed" (*vayishak*) are spelled identically, only their vowels differ. This is a beautiful allusion to the unity of good deeds and prayer, the integration needed for the full manifestation of Divine and human compassion.

In Kabbalah, the arousal of compassion by doing good deeds first, and then praying, refers to a situation where the initiator is represented by the "groom"—here Jacob—who draws God's energy from "above to below."

In the Song of Songs this order is actually reversed. There the "bride" —who represents the flow of energy from "below to above"—speaks, and therefore the "kiss" comes before the good deed, which is an offer of refreshment:[16]

> "Would you only be as a brother, having nursed from the breasts of my mother, I shall then find you outside and kiss you and no one will scorn me. I shall lead you and bring you to the house of my mother, you shall teach me, I shall give you to drink spiced wine from my choice pomegranates."[17]

In Kabbalah, the terms "bride" and "groom" are always relative, representing primordial forces present in both male and female. The "feminine" tends to pray first then act, whereas the "masculine" is more directed to acting first and then praying. In truth, both attitudes have their merits and their proper place.

Before Esther entered the inner chamber of the king uninvited, an act punishable by death, she asked all the Jews in Shushan to fast and pray with her for three days. (See the earlier explanation of the second dynamic of leadership for the full story.) Her efforts were ultimately successful, as is recorded in the Book of Esther and celebrated on the holiday of Purim.

But when the Israelites, trapped before the Sea of Reeds, cried out to God to save them from the approaching Egyptians, God told Moses: "Why cry to Me? Speak to the children of Israel that they go forward."[18]

Although both strategies have their time and place, we are taught that, since prayer is more potent when preceded and supported by acts of loving-kindness, this is the better path to pursue.

We see a further example of this in how Jacob—returning to the land of Israel after a twenty-year absence—coped with the threat of Esau's force of four hundred men arrayed against him. In response, Jacob sent gifts in order to facilitate peace, divided his camp in preparation for war, and only then prayed.[19] Our sages instruct us that Jacob's three-stage strategy is the model formula for Jewish leaders in all generations.

Through a lifetime of caring for others, the leader fine-tunes his ability to know the proper time and place for both action and prayer. The experience of compassion in his heart is ultimately a gift of God, creating an ongoing dynamic whereby the more he is compassionate, the more he draws down God's compassion. The result is Divine inspiration, one of the defining factors of a true leader.

Although one can be inspired in an almost infinite number of ways, prayer in both the formal and spontaneous sense is perhaps the most powerful vehicle for consciously achieving inspiration. Given the proper conditions, virtually any phenomenon can arouse inspiration, but these are indirect means to inspiration. Prayer is a direct means because it is directed to God, the source of all inspiration, and the result is, therefore, immediate and not delayed by intermediaries or detours.[20]

# THE ORIGIN OF INSPIRATION

The spirit of God shall rest upon him, the spirit of wisdom and understanding, the spirit of counsel and might, the spirit of knowledge and fear of God. And he will be inspired in the fear of God and he shall not judge after the sight of his eyes, nor decide after the hearing of his ears...[21]

This passage from the Book of Isaiah refers specifically to the origin of inspiration—"the spirit of God"—of the Messiah and by inference, to the spark of the Ultimate Leader in every Jew.[22]

In the phrase "the spirit of God," the Name of God used in the Hebrew original is the name associated with the attribute of compassion. This is God's essential four-letter name (known as the

Tetragrammaton) which we are forbidden to pronounce. The sages refer to it as "the Name of Compassion." Thus, the "spirit of God"-—that is, Divine inspiration—appears once more in conjunction with, and dependent upon, the attribute of compassion.

When we look at the second verse of this passage in Hebrew, we see that its first word, "and he will be inspired," is written *vaharicho*, which literally means "and he will apply his sense of smell." Therefore, the sages interpret this to mean that the Ultimate Leader will be inspired to judge by use of his sense of smell.[23] Though this may sound strange, consider that the common expression "something doesn't smell right," often employed to illustrate situations that feel intuitively wrong, alludes to the association between the sense of smell and judgment. Smell is connected to intuition and inspiration, both of which emanate from a super-conscious level above logic and reason. The Ultimate Leader will embody the consummate state of ongoing inspiration from God that will empower his judgment.

The well-known culmination of this prophecy from Isaiah comes a few verses later:

> ...for the earth shall be filled with the knowledge of God as the waters cover the sea.[24]

While "the spirit of God [that] will rest upon him" refers to an all-encompassing level of inspiration, it describes an individual experience, the experience of the Ultimate Leader himself. But "the earth shall be filled with the knowledge of God" refers to a climactic manifestation of inspiration encompassing all humanity, the "flood" of Divine knowledge that will cover the face of the earth "as the waters cover the sea." The role of the Ultimate Leader is to be the channel and priming force opening up God's infinite flow of inspiration to all the world. (Any spiritual leader who acts on a smaller stage nevertheless toils to become a proper conduit of Divine inspiration for his immediate followers and, even beyond, to all who come into contact with him.)

Isaiah describes the spirit of God as a "singular" spirit, while the spirit of wisdom is paired with understanding, the spirit of counsel with might, and the spirit of knowledge with the fear of God. This reflects the essential and absolute oneness of God in contrast to the apparent duality of creation and humanity. These pairs allude to a process that in Kabbalah is called "mating"—the ongoing spiritual balancing of the various forces and influences within the soul. To truly accomplish this requires God's assistance, compassion, and inspiration.

This prophecy of Isaiah is the most explicit reference to inspiration in the Bible; to capture the depth of its message it is necessary to analyze the many allusions contained in the Hebrew words, especially as they relate to the Biblical figure of Noah. In fact, in the story of Noah we can identify the first three of the four levels of inspiration mentioned by Isaiah, albeit in a state needing rectification. The fourth and final level, "the spirit of knowledge and fear of God," alludes to the culmination of Isaiah's prophecy quoted above, "for the earth shall be filled with the knowledge of God as the waters cover the sea." Though he possessed the latent potential to become the Ultimate Leader, Noah did not succeed in attaining this level—to flood the world with the spiritual knowledge of God. Had he done so, the physical destruction of the world by flood would have been avoided.[25]

"The spirit of God shall rest upon him," Isaiah states. The root of the Hebrew word for "rest" (*nach*)—which also means "descend" and "inspire"—is identical in its Hebrew spelling to *Noah*. The root of the word for "spirit" (*ruach*) is related to the word for "smell" (*reiach*). The root words for "smell" and "rest" are joined together in two important phrases or idioms relating to sacrifices offered in the Tabernacle in the desert and later in the Temple in Jerusalem, where the sacrifices are called a "pleasing aroma" (*reiach nichoach*) to God.[26] The very first time the phrase "pleasing aroma" appears in the Torah is after the great flood had subsided and Noah exited the ark:

> Then Noah built an altar to God and took of every clean animal and of every clean bird and offered burnt offerings on the altar. God smelled the pleasing aroma and God said in His heart, "I will not curse the ground again because of man..."[27]

The first time a word or phrase appears in the Torah is vital to understanding its significance. The first time the name Noah appears, we learn that its meaning is "rest."

> Lamech lived 182 years and had a son. And he called his name Noah saying, "This one will bring us rest from our work and the toil of our hands, from the ground which God had cursed."[28]

The "rest" that Noah brought was two-fold.

First, Noah is credited with inventing the plow,[29] which brought rest to weary men toiling to bring forth bread from the earth by the sweat of their brow. As a consequence of Adam's sin the ground had been "cursed," bringing only thorns and weeds when seeds were planted. According to tradition, the severity of the curse lasted only through the lifetime of Adam; Noah was born immediately after Adam's death and was instrumental through his inventiveness in causing the curse to abate, thereby giving rest to others.

The second "rest" that Noah brought was the promise he elicited from God not to curse the ground anew or destroy the earth again through another flood.[30]

The secret of the soul of Noah relates to the ultimate purpose of all creation—to come to a state of perfect rest and inspired consciousness, as Jews request in the blessing after a Shabbat meal: "May the Compassionate One cause us to inherit the day which will be completely Shabbat and a rest day for eternal life."[31]

Although Noah did not save his generation from the flood, he possessed leadership qualities; his goodness and the grace that he found in the eyes of God were sufficient to save himself—and potentially all humanity—from utter destruction:

> And God said, "I will blot out man whom I created from the face of the earth—from man to animal, to creeping things and to birds of the sky, for I regret that I created them." But Noah found grace in the eyes of God.[32]

His inability, though, to exhibit sincere compassion on his generation was considered a major failing that needed rectification.

It is related in the *Zohar* that after the floodwaters had subsided and Noah finally comprehended the extent of the destruction, he questioned how God could have done such a thing. God's response was one of incredulity:

> "You are a foolish shepherd. Now you say this?!
> Why did you not say this at the time I told you
> that I saw that you were righteous among your
> generation, or afterward when I said that I
> would bring a flood upon the people, or
> afterward when I said that you should build an
> ark? I constantly delayed and I said, 'When is he
> [Noah] going to ask for compassion for the
> world?'... And now that the world is destroyed,
> you open your mouth to cry before Me and to
> beseech Me?!" [33]

The sages debated whether Noah, had he been alive in the generation of Abraham, would have been considered especially outstanding or not. Some were of the opinion that had he lived among other holy men such as Abraham he would have been even greater than he had been in his own generation; others claimed he was good only in comparison to his wicked generation and had he lived at the time of Abraham he would have been thought of as quite ordinary.

The comparison with Abraham is not coincidental. When God revealed to Abraham His intention to destroy the evil cities of Sodom and Gomorrah, he pleaded that the cities be saved on the merit of the small minority of good people who might be living there.

Abraham's debate with God over the fate of Sodom and Gomorrah is as dramatic as a confrontation between God and a leader can be.

First the Torah tells us that God chose to include Abraham as a partner in His decision-making process:

> Now God had said, "Shall I conceal from
> Abraham what I am about to do? Abraham is to
> become a great and mighty nation and through
> him shall be blessed all the nations of the
> world."[34]

Having learned of the impending destruction, Abraham argued and pleaded that the cities should be saved if fifty good men live there.[35] Never forgetting his humility, he challenged God and found the Master of the Universe acceding to his requests:

> "Here I have begun to speak to my Master and I
> am but dust and ashes. But suppose they lack
> five of the fifty righteous? Will you destroy the
> whole city because of five. He [God] said, "I will
> not destroy if I find forty-five." He [Abraham]
> continued to speak to Him and said, "Suppose
> there are forty found there?" He [God] said, "I
> will not do it for the sake of the forty." He
> [Abraham] said, "Let not my Master show anger
> and I will continue to speak. Suppose thirty are
> found there?"[36]

Abraham stopped after winning a concession from God that the cities would not be destroyed if the minimal number of ten good men could be found among the evil population. But even ten could not be found, and, in the end, only Lot and his family were saved. Remarkably, it is from them that comes the lineage leading to Ruth—the model convert who was the great-grandmother of King David—and through King David ultimately to *Mashiach ben David.*

With his willingness to plead on behalf of the residents of these evil cities, Abraham began the process of rectifying Noah's inability to intercede for his generation. However, the complete rectification did not occur until the coming of Moses.[37]

Just before descending from Mt. Sinai with the two tablets on which were written the Ten Commandments, Moses was informed by God that, down below, the people had begun to worship the golden calf. God told him:

> "I have seen this people and behold they are a stiff-necked people. Now leave Me alone and My wrath will blaze against them and destroy them. I will then make you into a great nation."[38]

Another man might have been flattered by such a distinction, but Moses implored God to reconsider. In response to these arguments, the Torah relates, "God relented regarding the evil that He declared He would do to His people".[39]

After descending from Mt. Sinai and forcefully dealing with the situation, Moses ascended the mountain again, this time to beseech God to forgive the people. In what is considered the paradigm of the total dedication of the soul (*mesirut nefesh*), he declared:

> "I implore! This people has committed a grievous sin and made themselves a god of gold. And now if you would but forgive their sin, but if not, erase me now from this book that You have written."[40]

Interestingly, the Hebrew word for "erase me" (*mecheini*) is a permutation of *mei Noach*, "the waters of Noah." In Kabbalah,[41] we are taught that at that moment the blemish in the soul of Noah was rectified. Furthermore, these powerful words of Moses serve to instruct all future leaders as to the level of compassion and commitment needed to fulfill their appointed task.

Rabbi Menachem Mendel Schneersohn, the Lubavitcher Rebbe, taught that the pattern of all history—from the beginning of creation to the coming of the Messiah—is alluded to in the first ten generations of mankind from Adam to Noah, thus marking Noah as a potential Messiah, the Ultimate Leader.

Adam contained the potential of Ultimate Leadership while still in the Garden of Eden. This potential, which was lost when he ate from the Tree of Knowledge of Good and Evil, is alluded to in the teaching of the Ari who notes that the three Hebrew letters of the name Adam, are the first letters of Adam, David, and Messiah.

Of course, as has already been noted, had Noah been able to feel compassion for his generation, he might have realized the true spark of the Messiah within his soul. Nevertheless, he did merit to save humanity from utter destruction.

We are taught that "all sevenths are precious,"[42] and we see that the seventh generation following Adam was that of Chanoch of whom it is written: "And Chanoch walked with God, and then he was no more, for God had taken him."[43] The first two letters of the name Chanoch are the same as Noah but in reversed order, spelling the word for "grace" (*chen*), as in "And Noah found grace in the eyes of God."[44]

As there were ten generations from Adam to Noah, so were there ten generations following Noah to Abraham. The seventh generation from Abraham was that of Moses.[45]

And here we see a parallel between Chanoch (the seventh generation from Adam) and Moses (the seventh from Abraham). According to Kabbalah, in the world of souls, Chanoch was the spiritual mentor and teacher of Moses. Both of these souls were connected by their sense of selflessness, symbolized by the manner in which they left the world.

Regarding the death of Chanoch, it is written (as noted above): "and then he was no more for God had taken him." This is interpreted by the sages to mean that God saw that Chanoch was inclined to weaken spiritually as time progressed, despite his great goodness; therefore, God took him before his time. Tradition holds that he ascended to heaven where he was transformed into one of the loftiest of heavenly beings, the angel *Metatron.*

Concerning the death of Moses it is written: "And Moses, the servant of God died there, in the land of Moab, by the mouth of God... Moses was 120 years old when he died; his eye had not dimmed and his bodily strength had not diminished."[46] Moses was among a select few, who due to their spiritual purity, died by the "kiss" of God. As the verse indicates, Moses was in robust health until the time of his death. His death, like Chanoch's, was premature; it occurred only because his mission in this world had been completed.[47]

# NOAH AND THE FIVE DYNAMICS OF LEADERSHIP

When we examine the life of Noah, we see that despite certain limitations and failings, Noah possessed, albeit in a limited sense, all five dynamics of leadership described in this book. As discussed above, his sense of compassion—though flawed—was sufficient in God's eyes to save a remnant of humanity. His drive to achieve wholeness was manifest in his faithfulness in carrying out God's instructions to build an ark, gather a representative sample of the animal kingdom, and become the forerunner of a new world. Until our present day, the world is morally guided and bound by the universal code of ethics known as the "seven commandments of the children of Noah."[48]

His sense of compromise was put to the test during the time spent within the ark. Despite very difficult circumstances, he tended to all the needs of both his family and the animals, creating some semblance of order and balance.

His invention of the plow, a revolutionary advance for his time, and his ability to build an ark which served as the means to save life on earth, relate to the fourth dynamic of leadership, the drive for integration of technology and religion. And we see the fifth dynamic—a sense of folly—in his planting of a vineyard following the flood. As with some of his other traits, this sense of folly was not in a rectified state and it led him to becoming drunk and humiliated. The soul of Noah can thus be seen as a transitory figure, full of great potential, but in deep need of rectification.[49]

Let us now see what more we can learn from Noah about the third dynamic of leadership. Particularly, we find that Noah received from God three distinct commands relating to the ark—to build the ark, to enter the ark, and to leave the ark—and that each of these commands parallels the levels of inspiration we saw identified by Isaiah.

Noah was first commanded to build the ark. This stage relates to the all-encompassing inspiration—the "spirit of God" in Isaiah's words—that is meant to awaken compassion and the motivation to act. Noah's initial reaction was to fulfill God's directive to the letter of the law. He failed, however, to appreciate his power to arouse his generation to repent or his option to appeal to God's sense of compassion. Due to this serious lack, all of his subsequent stages of inspiration were incomplete as well.

Upon finishing the construction, Noah was commanded to take his immediate family and the animals and enter the ark, where they would be protected from the flood. Although the floodwaters were the agent for mass destruction, they also served to purify the world.[50] The paradoxical state of water both destroying and purifying is reflected in Jewish law, where water has the power to transfer spiritual impurity, as well as the unique power to purify the spiritually impure.

Entering the ark represents the second stage of inspiration: "the spirit of wisdom and understanding." On one level the experience of Noah in the ark was that of all reality being brought into one confined space. According to Kabbalah, the ark is the prototypical model of the Temple whose components, dimensions, and details symbolize the totality of both the material and spiritual worlds.[51]

On another level, the experience in the ark was one of hiding and waiting until the anger of God subsided. The Hebrew word for "wait/waiting" (*mechakeh*) is composed of the same letters as the word for "wisdom" (*chochmah*). Hassidism teaches that the three great sins of humanity—the sin of Adam and Eve, the sin of the golden calf, and the sin of David and Bathsheba—all involve impatience and the inability to wait for the proper time.

Had Adam and Eve waited for Shabbat, they would have been permitted not only to eat from the Tree of Knowledge of Good and Evil, but from the other special tree growing in the Garden of Eden, the Tree of Life as well. Had the generation of the desert waited only a short while longer, Moses would have descended from the mountain, and thus they would have avoided the grave sin of the golden calf. David and Bathsheba were destined to marry; had they waited for the right time, they would have avoided much trouble and anguish to themselves and others.[52]

The Hebrew word for "ark" (*teivah*) also means "word." The Ba'al Shem Tov, in one of his most important teachings,[53] allegorically saw Noah's ark as the vehicle of speech leading to redemption. Just as Noah was commanded to bring "all of reality" into the ark, so too are we directed to invest our entire being into the words of Torah and prayer.[54] When we bring the full spectrum of our intellectual, meditative, and emotional states into the words of Torah and prayer, we are able to ride upon the destructive floodwaters of this world and transmute them into purifying waters of redemption and inspiration.

Being hidden in the ark alludes to the "spirit of wisdom and understanding" and immersion in the inner dimensions of Torah.[55] In the Hassidic model of leadership, the potential leader first "hides" within the secret wisdom of the Torah, preparing himself to spread the understanding of those teachings at the proper time, and only then does he act.[56]

The crucial transition between preparation and action, as it relates to a leader, entails a deep understanding of the concept embodied in the statement: "we will do and we will hear."[57] In this one dramatic sentence, the Jews who were gathered at Mt. Sinai declared their total dedication to God, promising first to fulfill His commandments and only then to seek an understanding of what was demanded of them.

Despite this declaration, which has guided the Jewish people ever since, the human mind is naturally drawn to the more normative, logical statement of the sages, "great is learning that leads to action,"[58] which implies that one should first aim to understand and then to act upon that understanding.

In our present state of reality, understanding sparks the inspiration to act, but the reverse will be true in the Messianic era when the consciousness of "we will do and we will hear" will be truly revealed.

Indeed, another opinion of the sages—"Great [in itself] is the act"[59]—alludes to a higher consciousness wherein spontaneous action sparks inspiration from which, in turn, comes a "spirit of wisdom and understanding" that is infinitely higher than any insight that may have preceded the action.[60]

## A NEW WORLD

The third command received by Noah was to leave the ark:

> "Go forth from the ark—you and your wife, your sons and your son's wives with you. Every living being that is with you...order them out with you and let them increase on the earth and be fruitful and multiply on the earth."[61]

This command corresponds to the "spirit of counsel and might" in the verse from Isaiah.

The insulated environment of the ark was only a means to prepare human consciousness to experience the "new world" of the post-flood period. In addition to physically leaving the ark, the command implies leaving the confined mentality of the pre-flood world, ready to fulfill the directive to spread the wellsprings of wisdom to their farthest extremes. Even though the process of spreading wisdom conceptually begins in the ark, it remains confined by its very limited context. Only a new consciousness, outside the confines of logic and reason, is able to achieve the true expansion of Divine knowledge "like waters cover the sea," the culminating stage of inspiration.

The "spirit of counsel and might" complements the more intellectual level of the "spirit of wisdom and understanding."[62] Though usually the "spirit of wisdom and understanding" precedes the "spirit of counsel and might," sometimes, during extraordinary conditions when action is immediately mandated, the order is reversed. (This is similar to the alternating primacy of prayer and acts of kindness, as well as to the alternating primacy of action and understanding.) Also, the "spirit of counsel" precedes the "spirit of might" in order to regulate might and apply it in proper proportion to the situation at hand. If not, the danger exists of "breaking of the vessels," when an abundance of energy overwhelms a situation, causing destruction instead of rectification.

When Noah left the ark he was one of the few people to ever witness, in a literal sense, a "new world." In effect, that was the message of the command to leave the ark—to leave behind the "old world" consciousness and to build a new one.

Of all the widespread corruption of Noah's "old world," the sin most responsible for bringing the flood was rampant thievery, which created a climate of distrust and fear between people. This fear was magnified as the subtle threat of the flood hung over the generation like a dark cloud.

But when Noah left the ark God blessed him[63] that these fears would be a thing of the past, and further reassured him by establishing a new covenant:

> "And I will establish My covenant with you. Never again shall all flesh be cut off by the waters of the flood, and never again shall there be a flood to destroy the earth."[64]

The blessing and the covenant were meant to pave the way for man to begin anew, free of distrust and fear.

The flood occurred in the year 1656 of the Hebrew calendar. The generation of the Tower of Babel, years later, re-entered the "old world" mentality of fear by thinking the world was destined to collapse every 1656 years. In response, they began building a tower that would reach the heavens, somehow preventing this from occurring.

> And they said, "Come let us build us a city, and a tower with its top in the heavens, and let us make a name for ourselves, lest we be dispersed across the whole earth."[65]

Due to the existential threat they erroneously thought was facing them, they were overcome by fatalism. Ironically, the very displacement they feared became a self-fulfilling prophecy:

> And God dispersed them from there over the face of the whole earth, and they stopped building the city.[66]

The teachings of the Torah are eternal and its stories are archetypal in nature, forever repeating themselves in different guises and historic circumstances. In our times, the Holocaust parallels the destructive waters of the flood. For hundreds of years before World War II, Jews as a whole lived in a constant state of conscious or subconscious fear, due to their precarious status among the host nations. The forces of nationalism and revolution unleashed in Europe during the period of the Enlightenment added to the atmosphere of constant tension and conflict. Both sets of forces reached their tragic, climactic frenzy in the Holocaust.

Immediately following the end of World War II, Jewish sovereignty was renewed in the land of Israel, after two thousand years of determination and hope of an exiled people. This event, like the Holocaust, has no precedent in world history and parallels leaving the ark and the beginning of a "post-flood" reality. With the rebirth of Israel and the ingathering of the exiles, we witnessed the potential beginning of the fulfillment of the ancient covenant between God and the Jewish people, wherein God promised this land as an everlasting inheritance to His people, Israel. This corresponds to the covenant made by God with Noah immediately following the flood.

Although the threat of attack by hostile neighbors constantly hangs over Israel's very existence, the underlying message of the times for the Jewish people is to leave the pre-Holocaust period of constant fear and apprehension, and with great courage create a "new world," one that will hasten the Messianic era. For this to occur we need an enlightened leadership graced by God with the "spirit of counsel and might."

For the Jews, this time period closely resembles that of Noah, in that a tremendous leadership potential exists, as evidenced by the rebirth of Israel and the ingathering of the exiles. But, like Noah, the Jews of today appear to be falling short of grasping the ultimate opportunity.

Building a "new world" depends on not fearing the tragedies of the "old world." This does not mean being naive or careless, but trusting that God will not allow another "flood" or another Holocaust. To fully enter a new age, the Jewish people must forge a new consciousness, forcefully building a new world, and thus bringing the Messianic era closer by drawing the future into the present. In this moment, learning activates action; in the future, action will arouse inspiration.[67]

In the beginning stage of his leadership, the Ultimate Leader will be propelled by the dictum, "Great is learning that leads to action"—the epitome of the "spirit of wisdom and understanding." At a later stage, that dictum will be transformed into the fulfillment of "great [in itself] is the act"—the essence of the "spirit of counsel and might." His Divine appointment will initially create within him a vision and inner reality of a new world, free from paranoia and fear. His inner reality will eventually reflect outward to encompass the whole world.

As a teacher and leader, the Ultimate Leader, the Messiah, represents the collective potential of the Jewish people to be a source of great counsel and a "light unto the nations." One of the names by which the Messiah is called by Isaiah is a "wondrous giver of counsel." [68] The source of his counsel, as Isaiah notes elsewhere, is God Himself:

> "God, You are My God; I will exalt You; I will give thanks to Your Name for you have achieved wondrous counsels from afar in firm faith."[69]

"From afar" alludes to God's surrounding, transcendent light, perceptible to only the highest, unconscious point of faith in the soul, a point where one is ever ready to give oneself totally to God. This level of counsel emanates from far above the mind, appearing wondrous when grasped.[70]

The letters of the Hebrew word for "wondrous" (*pele*) are the same as the name of the first letter of the Hebrew alphabet, *alef*, only inverted. One of the meanings of the word *alef* is "teach."[71] *Alef* alludes to the level of wisdom and understanding, while its letters when inverted spell *pele*, alluding to an even higher "wondrous" level—the source of counsel and might.

When discussing the successive stages in a man's life, the 2nd century sage Yehudah ben Teima states: "a fifty-year-old can offer counsel."[72] In Kabbalah, the number fifty is always associated with the "fifty gates of understanding."[73] The fiftieth gate corresponds to the highest point of faith in the soul, the "unknowable head," as noted earlier. The forty-nine gates all correspond to the consciousness of "I know," whereas the fiftieth gate corresponds to the awareness that "I really don't know." On a number of occasions, when confronted with questions of which he was unsure, Moses, the greatest of all teachers, admitted that he did not know. The sages of the Talmud follow this example by admonishing: "Teach your tongue to say, 'I do not know,' lest you be led to lie."[74]

On a deeper level, it is taught in Hassidism that the fiftieth gate should not be seen as a separate state of consciousness, but should be experienced within all the other gates as well. This is derived from the commandment to count a measure of barley, the *omer*, each day during the seven weeks between the remembrance of redemption from Egypt on Passover and the giving of the Torah on Shavuot:

"And you shall count from the next day after the
rest day [Passover], from the day that you
brought the measure of the wave offering; there
are to be seven weeks, until the day after the
seventh week, you are to count fifty days…" [75]

The redemption from Egypt and the freedom
accompanying it were but the means to an end—the receiving of
the Torah. Therefore, each day of the counting and each gate of
understanding includes in it the fiftieth day and the fiftieth gate,
the ever-present culminating goal. This lesson serves as a clear
directive to a leader—always have your ultimate goals
accompanying you and leading your every step.

The level of counsel emanates from the fiftieth gate, the
aspiration of the future. This level is even beyond prophetic insight
flowing from wisdom and understanding, as Isaiah says:

No eye has seen, besides You, God, that which
will be done for those who wait for Him. [76]

The Hebrew word for "wait/waiting" (*mechakeh*) is
composed of the same letters as the word for "wisdom" (*chochmah*)
as mentioned above. Though the eyes of wisdom cannot clearly
see the World to Come, those who wait for God's counsel can
glimpse a vision of the fiftieth gate, as it is drawn momentarily into
the present.

For those who can glimpse that vision, the waiting is not
passive. Rather it means being actively involved in the present, in
order to take advantage of every opportunity to leave the ark of
the present world, and, through a "spirit of counsel and might,"
create a new age.

# 5

# Fourth Dynamic

## THE DRIVE FOR INTEGRATION

Every true leader has a plan of how to return the world to good—to rectify the rampant violence and immorality—so that the society we live in will become a Godly place. This entails a total involvement in current affairs and a broad knowledge of the arts and sciences in order to uplift them to their Divine source. This drive to integrate the secular with the holy is the fourth dynamic of leadership.

Before delving into the principles underlying this dynamic, it is important to explore further the relationship between Israel and the other nations touched upon in the introduction. The culminating goal of the Ultimate Leader—to unite all humanity to recognize the one God—depends on Israel and the nations fulfilling their appointed tasks. The Torah states that all peoples of the world derive from seventy primary nations, the seventy primary descendants of Noah as enumerated in the Book of Genesis.[1] The rectification of these nations occurs through the fulfillment of the seven commandments given to the descendants of Noah, the "universal religion" stretching back even further in time to Adam and Eve.

The Noahide commandments prohibit:

- worshiping any entity other than one God
- blaspheming God's Name
- murder
- theft
- certain types of sexual relations
- eating meat taken from a live animal

Additionally, they prescribe the establishment of a court system to ensure a just society based on these laws.

Though some of the details vary, the majority of the Noahide commandments were later included in the Ten Commandments and their moral guidance has greatly influenced all mankind. In our day, it is important for the world not only to recognize the moral authority of these seven commandments, but their source in Torah as well.

The number seven is rich in meaning and is associated with the lower seven of the ten *sefirot*—the Divine channels through which God makes His Presence known in the world. These lower seven are considered the *sefirot* of the heart and correspond to the seventy archetypal nations. In contrast, Israel is associated with the upper three, the *sefirot* of the mind.[2] Though the intellect must always be connected to, and at times draw inspiration and guidance from the emotions,[3] its main task and responsibility is to lead.

In *The Kuzari*,[4] a classic book of medieval Jewish philosophy, Israel is described as the heart and the other nations as the limbs of the body. The metaphor of the heart pumping sustenance to the body parallels that of the head directing the heart.

Hassidism explains the difference in these parallel images as that between exile and redemption. While in exile, the Jewish people, due to circumstances, function more like the heart, feeling the suffering of the world, and, in allegorical and mystical fashion, suffering for the world. (Indeed, many Jewish and non-Jewish authors have described the Jews as the "conscience of the world.") But in a redemptive state, the Jewish people will assume their more natural role as the head, leading the world to a new age.

In the 18th century—when the Enlightenment made it possible for Jews for the first time to operate within general society—it was amazing to see how quickly they rose to the top of so many professions, as well as in the arts, sciences, and politics of their host countries.

Since all souls, both Jewish and non-Jewish, are connected at their ultimate source, when one level elevates itself, all levels are drawn upward as well. The natural inclination of the Jewish people is to elevate themselves to the level of mind and leadership, which naturally uplifts the entire world.

The source of the Jewish soul is rooted in the essence of God. Its purpose is to inspire the world with a deep, transcendent perspective of reality. This relates to our earlier discussion (see the first dynamic of leadership: the art of compromise) that reality, when experienced from a higher dimension, reconciles apparent paradoxes and unites all plurality in essential oneness. When this consciousness is fully implanted in the world, all the nations will be able to fulfill the seven Noahide commandments in an inspired state.

Being inspired when performing a commandment is an ideal not only for the future, but a goal that should be pursued on a daily basis. One of the original goals of the leaders of the Hassidic movement was to re-instill in the Jewish people a joyous and deeply spiritual attitude towards each and every religious obligation. A person who performs a ritual by rote can be likened to a slave who, motivated by fear of the master's punishment, takes no pleasure in his or her actions. In contrast, a person who seeks to fulfill a commandment from love can be likened to a child of the master who actually feels the pleasure inherent in every action done on behalf of the master/father.[5]

Though fulfillment of a commandment is an emotional experience, it is enriched when preceded by proper, intellectual meditation and intent. Each action is intended to connect the individual directly to God, infusing both body and soul with tremendous life force and pleasure.

The purpose of all the commandments is identical with the goal of a true leader—to uplift the physical and unite it with the spiritual. Acting by rote drains away all the viable potential, leaving only an empty shell.

For Israel to be a "light unto the nations" it has to channel Torah as the source of God's light in the world. Serving God by rote not only does not inspire, it drives people to look for spirituality from sources other than Torah. This is especially true today within Jewish communities everywhere. First and foremost, the task of the Jews is to inspire other Jews to see the beauty and relevance of Torah today. Only then will other nations accept with love its universal message of brotherhood, equality, peace, and compassion.

Due to historical circumstances, Jews for the last two thousand years have not been in a position to teach openly the seven commandments of Noah (nor their inner meaning) to the nations. The tremendous influence the Jewish people have had on all aspects of religion, culture, and society has been more a result of osmosis than of a conscious decision. Only now, with a restored national home and acceptance as equal citizens in most countries, is there an atmosphere where Jews can begin consciously to choose to fulfill a true leadership role. A Jewish leader today must inspire the whole Jewish people to become what God intended for them from the time of the Exodus:

> "And you shall be to Me a nation of priests, and a holy people."[6]

Fulfillment of the commandments in an inspired fashion demonstrates to others that the Torah is not merely a body of rules to live by (lest in a lawless society people "swallow each other up"); it is a powerful spiritual vehicle through which we learn how to communicate directly with God on both a personal and universal level.[7]

The basic relationship between Israel and the nations can also be viewed through the teachings of the Ba'al Shem Tov outlined earlier—that all spiritual growth and Divine service unfolds in a three-stage process of "submission, separation, and sweetening." The initial stage of "submission" entails the Jewish people's humble acceptance of their Torah responsibilities, including becoming a "light unto the nations."

The next stage is highly paradoxical, for in order to realize the consummate stage of the unity of mankind in the service of God, an intermediate level of "separation" is needed.

Throughout history the Jewish people have maintained a separate identity, either by choice or by default, due to other peoples' refusal to accept them as equals on any level. Every attempt to assimilate among the nations has brought disaster in its wake, as any student of Jewish history knows.

The pagan prophet Balaam correctly prophesied that Israel would be "…a nation that dwells in solitude and will not be reckoned among the nations."[8] The state of separateness has been a source of blessing and curse—a blessing in that only in this way has Israel been able to maintain its unique, essential nature and thereby greatly influence the world, albeit in a manner not always immediately recognizable; and a curse in that it has prevented the other nations from fulfilling their true mission of drawing close to Israel and Torah.

However, the stage of "separation," though paradoxical, is indispensable to the overall unfolding of God's ultimate plan for humanity. Even after all the nations recognize the source of light emanating from the Jewish people, there will still need to be a separation. At that point though, the sense of separateness actually will motivate non-Jews to either want to convert or to draw closer by adopting the seven Noahide commandments.

When this spiritual arousal will reach and encompass all of humanity, part of the non-Jewish world will convert in full to Judaism, while the remaining part will accept its Torah-obligations and thereby merit to the status of "resident foreigner" (*ger toshav*). Non-Jews possessing the latter status are welcomed to the land of Israel and the Jewish people are required to care for them.[9] This is the stage of "sweetening" that the Ultimate Leader will reveal to the whole world.

The task of the Ultimate Leader is to unite the world in common purpose, transcending all differences between peoples. As the nations are inspired to fulfill their own unique purpose, they will become like an orchestra "conducted" by the Ultimate Leader to create, from a multitude of instruments, a beautiful and harmonious symphony.

# SOURCE OF WISDOM

Maimonides[10] states that if we want to know more about God we should look closely at the world around us where God's imprint is encoded in every detail of nature. The numerical value of the Hebrew Name of God that appears in the Genesis story of creation (*Elokim*) is the same as that of the Hebrew word for "nature" (*hateva*, 86). This Name of God appears in the creation account thirty-two times, alluding to the thirty-two pathways of wisdom spoken of in Kabbalah.

The human quest to understand the world around us has led to wisdom in many areas of life and in a multitude of intellectual disciplines; it is particularly evident in the scientific and technological revolutions of the last three centuries. A Jew, and especially a leader, should not be afraid to acknowledge and take advantage of these advancements but, quite the opposite, should seek to find their source in Torah, as the sages proclaim:

> Turn it [the Torah] over and turn it over again,
> for everything is in it...[11]

According to Kabbalah, the rectification of the physical world occurs through returning sparks of holiness at present entrapped in the "wisdoms" of the world to their source in Torah.[12] When the physical source of all earthly phenomena returns to its spiritual root, it is thus redeemed. By taking Albert Einstein's discovery—that all matter in essence is pure energy—one step further, we see that the unification of secular knowledge and Torah wisdom reveals that all energy in essence emanates from one God. Einstein intuited this while trying in the last years of his life to develop a unified field theory, which remains to this day the ultimate goal of modern physics.

The leader works ceaselessly to reveal a "unified field" of immediate experience to those around him or her, wherein secular and holy, physical and spiritual are all seen to be manifestations of one energy, God.[13]

## PRIMORDIAL DUST

"All go to one place; all are of the dust and all return to dust," states King Solomon in Ecclesiastes.[14]

Hidden in King Solomon's wisdom we may find an allusion to an important scientific theory of our day—that of the "Big Bang."[15] Modern astronomers believe that following this cataclysmic event, there began a process of formation of stars and galaxies from "primordial dust." They posit that in these initial stages just two elements—hydrogen and helium—existed. Only as stars solidified did they become "factories" for more elements; then, when these ancient stars exploded, they seeded the cosmos with the new elements needed for a developing universe.

"Primordial dust" represents the totality of energy in the universe. Scientists now purport that all life on earth is in essence "star dust." These modern discoveries only confirm the statement by the sages made more than two thousand years ago: "All comes from dust, even the sun."[16]

We are taught in Kabbalah that the four cardinal elements of fire, air, water and earth/dust relate to the ten *sefirot* in the following manner:

- fire to *chochmah* ("wisdom")

- air to *binah* ("understanding")

- water to the six emotive *sefirot*, namely,
  *chesed* ("loving-kindness"),
  *gevurah* ("fortitude"), *tiferet* ("beauty"),
  *netzach* ("victory"), *hod* ("thanksgiving" or
  "glory") and *yesod* ("foundation")

- earth or dust to the last of the emotive
  *sefirot*, *malchut* ("kingship")

The connection of dust to *malchut* alludes to the very rectification of the leader that we have been discussing in this chapter. For only when *malchut*, the lowest of the *sefirot*, has mastered the material aspect of "dust"—by means of the spiritual attribute of existential lowliness innate to a true king—will kingship merit to wear the "crown" (*keter*) of the highest *sefirah*, symbolizing the epitome of the spiritual realm.[17]

We are further taught in Kabbalah that dust/earth and the other primary elements have essential and secondary qualities.

Their correspondences are as follows:

| element | essential quality | secondary quality |
|---------|-------------------|-------------------|
| fire | hot | dry |
| air | wet | hot |
| water | cold | wet |
| dust | dry | cold |

Dry and cold—the qualities of dust—connote death. Yet, we know that plants, animals, and human beings all derive their sustenance from the power of life and growth innate in the dust of the earth. This apparent paradox is reconciled by the apex of God's creation, the human being, who is capable of bridging these two opposite yet essentially unified realities of life and death—the spiritual and the physical.

This is spelled out in the account of creation:

> Now all the trees of the field were not yet on the earth and all the herbs had as yet not sprouted, for God had not caused it to rain on the earth, and there was no man to work the soil.[18]

Rashi[19] explains:

> And for what reason had it not rained? Because there was no man to work the soil and none to recognize the goodness of rain; and when man came and knew that the rains were needed for the world, he prayed for rain and it fell, and the trees and the grasses sprouted.

The Hebrew words for "man/human being" (*adam*) and "earth" (*adamah*) are identical except for the final, feminine *hei* of the word for "earth." This alludes to the concept of "mother earth" and the "male-female" attraction between humanity and the earth from which it is nourished.[20]

The numerical values of the words for the essential and secondary qualities of dust—dry (*yavesh*, 312) and cold (*kar*, 300)—equal together the numerical value of the word for "covenant" (*brit*, 612). The first covenant God made with Abraham, even before the covenant of circumcision, was the covenant binding the

Jewish people to the land of Israel forever. History has shown that no power can permanently separate the Jewish people from its land. In the time of exile the connection was maintained by daily prayers for a return to Israel and by nurturing the great desire to at least be buried in the land, which many over the generations were, in fact, able to do.

In modern days, great numbers of Jews have returned, in their lifetime to their historical homeland to live and grow. Motivated by the deep yearning of all the generations of exile, the Jews came home to build their land and establish therein a sovereign state. Indeed, the land responded to the overture of the people—for the first time in two thousand years it began to blossom.

Ages ago, the sages spoke of the time when the land would once again be transformed from barren desert to a fruitful "paradise" as one of the portents for the coming of the Messiah. [21]

This phenomenon reflects the interdependency of the physical and the spiritual. When physical reality is disconnected from the spiritual, it is "barren" and empty of real meaning, but when it is transformed into a vessel for the Divine, it becomes fruitful and full of life.

In the words of the *Zohar,* until the final redemption, "the *Shechinah* [i.e. God's Presence] lies in the dust," [22] and it is the mission of the Jews to restore the *Shechinah* to glory.

In general, the term *Shechinah* is used synonymously with the term "the Congregation of Israel" (*Knesset Yisrael*), meaning the spiritual source of all the souls of Israel. The redemption of the *Shechinah* in its fullest sense will occur in the land of Israel when the dust itself and all it symbolizes is infused with its full spiritual potential and with God's Presence, ultimately yielding continual renewal and everlasting life.

# TECHNOLOGY, MUSIC AND ART

The Hassidic masters speak of certain great souls who had a sense for the physical world, meaning they had a special connection to the "dust" of the physical.[23] The Ultimate Leader will likewise have this special "sense," which in contemporary terms translates into a deep connection to science and the technological advances that are changing the very nature of life on earth. It has been widely discussed in recent years that many of the prophecies regarding the Messiah make most sense in a world that has turned into a "global village." It is beyond the scope of this book to delve extensively into this meaningful subject, but two examples might help to clarify this point.

For the Ultimate Leader to reach the entire world with his message and unite all peoples in the knowledge and service of the one God would require a system of communication that would allow him global access. Until recently this was not a feasible reality, but with the varied methods of instantaneous communication available to us now, this is no longer out of the realm of possibility.[24] Theoretically, he could speak to the entire world on "live" broadcast, thereby creating true world unity.

Overcoming hunger is another example. Until just 150 years ago there could be a major famine in one part of the world and distant countries would not hear of it until years later. Even if there had been the ability to disseminate the calls for help more quickly, in practical terms, relief could not have reached the stricken for months. Today, major natural disasters are reported worldwide in a matter of minutes and relief efforts are mounted immediately.

Technology, if properly harnessed, can be used for the most spiritual of purposes. On the simplest level, technology frees people to pursue activities leading to a higher consciousness. The development of technology in our day parallels Noah's invention of the plow (which we discussed earlier), both serving to rectify the "curse" of Adam to earn a livelihood by the sweat of his brow.

An inspired leader is well aware of this; he shows interest and concern not only in his followers' spiritual development but understands that the spiritual will blossom if the practical/material realm is in order as well.

While science and technology are two important aspects of the material realm, music and the visual arts are no less so.

Music has been a source of comfort to the Jewish people throughout their many exiles, inspiring a rich tradition of music for nearly every occasion. The visual arts on the other hand were for the most part limited to ritual art.

Only the Temple represents the visual arts in their full splendor, combining all creative expression in a unified vision. The Tabernacle in the desert, and later, the Temple in Jerusalem, symbolized not only the microcosm of the created universe but a holy space where God revealed, in a greater degree than anywhere else, His glory on earth. The destruction of the Temple represents the diminished spiritual vision of the arts and its rebuilding will be accompanied by a burst of creative artistic energy.

Both science and art, according to Kabbalah, have their ultimate source in the unconscious realm of *keter* ("crown"), the highest of the ten *sefirot*. But when revealed in the world, science must express itself through the intellect (i.e., the conscious) to be understood, whereas art always maintains its connection to the super-conscious sphere. In fact, the more subtle the artist's connection to the mysterious and intangible strata of the soul, the greater the work of art becomes. Science deals in clear and precise terms; its accomplishments appear as the workings of human beings. In contrast, art and music reveal the more indefinable awareness of God's grace in the soul and bring with them a recognition that an artistic creation is indeed a "gift" from God. [25]

# INTEGRATION

There is a unique grace found in every Jewish soul, eliciting God's continual compassion upon it. This innate aspect of soul, which should naturally reveal itself in every realm of existence, is still to a great extent in a state of exile. Detached from Torah, Jews everywhere are copying foreign cultures, blurring the innate and refined sense of science and art present within their souls.

It is the role of the contemporary leader to encourage the redemption of both science and art by revealing their source and unity in Torah. This entails demonstrating the true purpose of science and art, which is to reveal God's Presence and His will in every aspect of life and at every level of consciousness.

A numerical gem, supporting the ideas thus far presented, is found when adding the numerical values of the Hebrew words for "art" (*omanut*, 497) and "science" (*mada*, 114); these equal the numerical value of the word *Torah* (611). The word for "art" is closely related to the word for "faith" (*emunah*), the highest level of the super-conscious found in the *sefirah* of *keter* ("crown"), and the ultimate source of inspiration for all creative aspects of the soul. The word for "science" is closely related to the *sefirah* of *da'at* ("knowledge"), the culmination of the three conscious *sefirot* of intellect: *chochmah* ("wisdom"), *binah* ("understanding"), and *da'at* ("knowledge").

In certain respects, the above numerical equivalent is one of the future, when the secular worlds of art and science will not hide spirituality but will actually be converted into vehicles for powerful revelations of Divinity. This idea relates to our earlier discussion of how, in the future, action itself will be the source of inspiration, as opposed to the present reality where learning directs action. As the Messianic era approaches, the Torah will more and more be equated with the spontaneous sense of beauty and thirst for knowledge that is innate to the Jewish soul.

This phenomenon is clearly seen in the recent explosion of books and teachings that reveal Torah wisdom and its relevance to a gamut of scientific disciplines and contemporary professions. Recent discoveries in the area of quantum physics and cosmology now begin to approach the Torah's account of creation. Computers are probing the incredible mathematical structure and "codes" hidden in the Torah. Modern psychology has developed a language for describing the human personality and consciousness known for ages in Jewish tradition. Torah law, custom, and insights are now being recognized as valuable instruments and guidelines for an array of present-day difficulties and situations such as those involving the environment, education, sexuality, medical ethics, community structure, the legal system, etc.

In addition, there is enormous worldwide interest in finding meaning beyond the impersonal and alienating aspects of modern life and culture. This has led to a renewal of interest by Jews and non-Jews alike in the Jewish mystic tradition as embodied in Kabbalah and Hassidism. In a time when many are groping for a sense of purpose and moral guidelines in a rapidly changing world, the Torah stands out as a beacon of light and sanity for all humanity.

As the world becomes more advanced technologically, it is experiencing a paradox inherent in the nature of creation itself. In one sense, our physical universe reveals God's creative power and will. In another sense, though, the physical world serves as a curtain hiding His true infinite essence from a finite world not really prepared for such direct Divine experience. [26] This is seen in the fact that the Hebrew word for "world" (*olam*) derives from the same root as the word for "hiddenness" (*he'elem*). A well-known idiom employed by the sages to express this apparent paradox is: "He is the Place of the world but the world is not His place."

In a similar manner, the high-tech knowledge of today reveals and yet hides God's Presence in the world. After the inception of the Messianic era, the curtain preventing direct Divine experience will be slowly lifted in accordance with each soul's ability to integrate God's light. "Mother earth" will then give birth to spiritual pleasures we cannot at present even imagine. The true essence of the Creator will reveal itself in every point of the physical creation as the wellsprings of nature generate higher and higher levels of consciousness. Physical beauty at that time will become synonymous with spiritual beauty and wisdom; and technology properly harnessed and channeled will assist human spiritual development and refinement.

The spiritual light to be revealed in the Messianic era is called in mystical texts a "new" light. According to Kabbalah, this light comes from even above the "higher darkness," a term used to describe God's infinite potential to create, the "nothing" preceding the "something" of creation. Only in the Messianic era will this light, hidden within the very essence of God, break forth. An allusion to the unbounded joy of this revelation is captured in the hopeful prayer: "Shine a new light upon Zion, and may we all soon merit to enjoy its brightness."

It is the task of the true leader to draw this new light into our contemporary world and reveal how all reality is a fitting vessel for the revelation of God's very essence. The more a true Torah-based perspective is transmitted in a language the modern world can understand and respect, the more Torah is shown to encompass and relate to the here-and-now, and the more readily the message will be received and accepted.

In this regard, every Jew can make a significant contribution within his or her own immediate sphere of influence. Each ripple in the water has a power and momentum to create ever greater circles of spiritual movement until the "critical mass" is reached to break through the barrier or "firmament" that divides the "higher waters" (the Divine wisdom of the Torah) from the "lower waters" (the wisdom inherent in the arts and sciences).

In Kabbalah, the "higher waters" symbolize the male seed, while the "lower waters" symbolize the female seed. Their union impregnates the consciousness of all reality with the awareness that God's absolute unity is reflected equally in spirit and body.[27]

# 6

# Fifth Dynamic

## A SENSE OF FOLLY

The last of our five dynamics—a sense of humor or "holy folly"—is by its very nature the most paradoxical and enigmatic of all the qualities required of a true leader. The ability to display a good sense of humor, and, at the appropriate times, even a little foolishness in the right proportion to wisdom and dignity, mirrors the Creator's capacity to integrate and unify seemingly opposite states of reality.

We will introduce here three different perspectives to the application of folly as found in the Bible and the Jewish Oral Tradition, and then proceed to explain each in detail:

1) Any leader must on occasion apply severity in order to punish wrongdoing. As a result, those responsible are awakened, while those witnessing or hearing of the punishment are impelled to heed the warning. The tendency to punish, though, actually runs against the grain of the ideal leader, and therefore represents folly in relation to his own soul in that it actually hurts him as much as, if not more than, the person he is punishing.

2) There are times when a leader makes a fool of himself or even feigns insanity—as in the case of King David—in order to redeem a situation or even save his own life. In these extreme circumstances a leader must be able to employ a temporary strategy totally foreign to his essential nature for the sake of a higher good.

3) A touch of foolishness when used to awaken laughter and joy in others can generate a spiritually conducive atmosphere, opening channels for deeper rapport and unity among people.

These three manifestations of folly correspond to the three stages of spiritual development and Divine service as taught by the Ba'al Shem Tov and as explained earlier—"submission, separation, and sweetening."

"Submission" relates to the humility of soul engendered by punishment in both the leader and the recipient. "Separation" relates to the refinement resulting from the leader's ability to play the fool, as will be explained. "Sweetening" occurs when "holy folly" leads to joy and happiness.

## FOLLY AND PUNISHMENT

King Solomon, the wisest of all men, alluded to the characteristic of folly in a puzzling verse:

> Death-flies stink, yet they ultimately express fragrant oil; more precious than wisdom, than honor, is a little foolishness.[1]

This verse, as understood by the Midrash, relates to three specific cases of a leader using punishment.

The first case noted is that of Korach, who, when the Israelites wandered in the desert, challenged the right of Moses to lead the people.[2]

After a number of futile attempts to make peace with Korach, Moses told the people:

> "If as all men die [that is, naturally] will these men [Korach and his followers] meet their deaths ...then God has not sent me. [But] if God will create a new creation, and the earth will open its mouth and swallow them along with all their belongings, and they will go down alive to the grave, then you will know that these men have angered God."[3]

As he finished his words the earth opened up and swallowed up the rebels, thus confirming Moses' Divine appointment. The punishment also served to convince Korach of his mistaken judgment, and as he descended into the abyss, he was heard to confirm Moses' authority, thus metamorphosing "evil smelling" words into "fragrant oil."

Even greater than the prophecy of Moses was his sense of folly in asking God to "create a new creation," a request that on the surface defied logic and ran counter to his usual humbleness. But he must have felt that the situation required drastic measures if he were to bring Korach to repent and confirm his right to lead the people.

The second case referred to in the Midrash involves King David.[4] Doeg and Achitofel led a campaign of malicious slander against David, challenging not only his right to be king but his very Jewishness.[5] David, feeling betrayed, prayed to God to bring them down to the pit of destruction. It was this prayer that ultimately motivated them to change their attitude and repent.

The last case takes place in the days of Elijah the prophet.[6] In order to turn the Jewish people away from idol worship, Elijah challenged the priests of the idol Ba'al to a contest to prove who is the real God. The contest would pit Elijah against the 450 priests: each side would offer a sacrificial bull to their deity and whichever deity sent a fire from heaven to consume the offering in full sight of the people would be accepted as the true God. After nearly a full day of trying, the 450 priests could not induce Ba'al to act and their sacrifice sat rotting on the altar. All the while, Elijah mocked them:

> "Shout louder! After all, he is a god, but he may
> be in conversation, he may be detained, or he
> may be on a journey, or perhaps he is asleep and
> will wake up."[7]

As the day neared its end, Elijah prepared his own sacrifice, dousing it with water so it would be even more difficult to set aflame. He then offered one short prayer and immediately a fire came down from heaven and consumed not only the animal carcass but the wood and stones of the altar. The gathered multitude responded in awe, openly acknowledging the oneness of God.

The threat of punishment to the loser was implicit and pervaded the whole proceedings; indeed, at the close, Elijah ordered the priests of Ba'al seized and brought down into the valley of Kishon where they were executed.

The thread linking these three applications of King Solomon's verse is that punishment, or even the threat of retribution, effected a repentance that wisdom could not achieve. In addition, we see an allusion to "holy folly" in the case of Moses setting up a situation in which God had to "create a new creation," and in the case of Elijah concocting a "contest of the gods." Here, folly manifests itself as wisdom emanating from above normative reason.

Another similarity found in all three cases is the theme of descent. Korach descended into the abyss; David prayed to bring his enemies down to the pit of destruction; and Elijah brought the false priests of Ba'al down to the valley to be killed. Hassidism holds that strong words of constructive rebuke, even without any punitive action, have the power to "bring down" the evil inclination and awaken repentance.[8] The same result, if not more, can be seen when action accompanies oral rebuke.

Another verse in Proverbs written by King Solomon— "Also punishment for a righteous person [*tzadik*] is not good..."[9]— appears to contradict the above Midrashic interpretation that points to the positive aspects of punishment.

King Solomon's use of the phrase "not good" reminds us of the first appearance of these words in the Book of Genesis when God declares that "It is not good for man to be alone."[10] (This led to the creation of Eve to be Adam's wife.) The correlation between these two verses alludes to the *tzadik* also being alone, in that he must "divorce" himself from the one he is punishing. In so far as he endeavors to have a deep soul connection with everyone he contacts, it is as if he is "married" to that person, but when forced to dispense punishment, he feels existentially alone and this causes him great pain. Even knowing that the punishment will in the long run be beneficial does not mitigate the negative reaction the *tzadik* experiences.[11]

Similarly, punishment is hurtful to the very being of the Jewish leader inasmuch as all Jewish souls are connected; nevertheless, in order to ultimately sweeten reality, the leader must be willing to punish despite the painful personal toll.

In the three cases discussed above, Moses, David, and Elijah were all willing to exact punishment for the sake of the public good and for the sake of the repentance the punishments inspired. As a result, the people's belief in the Torah of Moses, the kingship of David, and the realization of the oneness of God at the time of Elijah, were all strengthened.

To elevate the intrinsic sense of caring for others above personal needs or desires requires taking the self out of one's center of focus, or in the idiom of Hassidism, "setting one's self aside." Rabbi Nachman of Breslov described this action as "augmenting the honor of heaven, while simultaneously decreasing one's own personal honor."[12]

In conclusion, we can see that the first manifestation of folly also follows the three stages of spiritual growth as taught by the Ba'al Shem Tov. The stage of "submission" is the effect punishment has on the leader; the impression on his or her soul remains long after the momentary submission experienced by the recipient of the punishment. "Separation" occurs as the person being punished is now able to differentiate between good and evil. "Sweetening" is achieved through sincere repentance, the purpose the leader intended in exercising the punishment in the first place.

Although this expression of the dynamic of folly contains all three stages, it is most associated with "submission," as manifest in the subjugation of the evil inclination, the neutralization of ego and the subjugation of the leader's own tendencies for the benefit of others.

The sages taught that "No one commits a sin unless a [temporary] spirit of foolishness enters him."[13] Recognizing this truth, the leader fights folly with folly. In this sense, one leads others by subjugating one's own interests for the good of the whole—the paradigm of submission in the soul. The essence of leadership is thus revealed in one who learns self-submission in order to serve both God and man.

## FOLLY AS INSANITY

The second manifestation of the dynamic of folly—feigning insanity—is based on the story of David, who, when fleeing from the wrath of King Saul, was forced to pretend that he lost his mind in order to escape from Achish, the king of Gat. The Midrash reveals the background to this fascinating story:

> David said to the Holy One: "All that You have made is beautiful, and wisdom is the most beautiful of all … but insanity that You created, what beauty is there in it for You? For example, when a man walks in the market and he drools over his clothes and children run after him and people make fun of him, is this beautiful to You?" The Holy One said to David: "You complain about the injustice of insanity; by your life you will need it."

Shortly thereafter, David had to flee for his life. The only place of refuge was Gat, a Philistine city-state whose inhabitants were the sworn enemies of Israel. Indeed, the bodyguard of the king was the brother of Goliath whom David had slain. Suspicious of the reasons for David's arrival, the advisors to the king recommended he kill David now and ask questions later. Terrified, David pretended to be mad; he "scratched on the doors of the gate and let his spittle run down his beard."[14] Seeing this behavior, the king—who had a mad wife and daughter—exclaimed: "Do I lack madmen, that you bring this one to display madness in front of me?" Thus, David's life was spared and he was allowed to leave Gat and escape to a nearby cave.

Realizing that even madness has a purpose, King David composed one of his most famous Psalms: "I will bless You at every moment; His praise shall be constantly in my mouth..."[15]

David's realization that every psychological state is useful in its right time is developed further by his son Solomon, who wrote: "For everything there is a season and a time for every purpose under heaven."[16]

In the passage that follows, various elements of life are enumerated, each one useful in its appropriate time:

> A time to be born, and a time to die; a time to plant, and a time to pluck up that which is planted. A time to kill, and a time to heal; a time to break down, and a time to build up. A time to weep, and a time to laugh; a time to mourn, and a time to dance. A time to cast away stones, and a time to gather stones together; a time to embrace, and a time to refrain from embracing. A time to seek, and a time to lose; a time to

keep, and a time to cast away. A time to rend,
and a time to sew; a time to keep silence, and a
time to speak. A time to love, and a time to hate;
a time of war, and a time of peace.[17]

In all, twenty-eight "times" are recorded, the number
associated with a lunar month, which is made up of four basic
seven-day quarters of the moon. The waxing and the waning of the
moon thus represent the full cycle of time.[18]

King David discovered that there was even a time for
madness. The more mysterious part of this story, however, is why
David's insanity saved him and how is it relevant to us today. In
examining the Kabbalah's answer, we must keep in mind that
David is the forerunner and prototype of the Ultimate Leader and
all of his actions, as recorded in the Bible, allude to deep spiritual
truths and archetypal historical patterns.

The first of those truths relates to the Ari's explanation of
the primordial "breaking of the vessels" which scattered holy
sparks throughout creation. As noted in our discussion of the
fourth dynamic of leadership, it is the primary mission of the
Jewish people to search out, uplift, and redeem these holy sparks.
The role of a true leader is to be in the forefront of these efforts,
ever aware of revealing holiness, especially in areas and situations
where it would be least expected.

It will be the final mission of the Ultimate Leader to
penetrate into the very depths of unrectified reality where evil
predominates, in order to liberate sparks of holiness and return
them to their rightful source. These attempts are fraught with
spiritual and physical danger, as alluded to in Proverbs: "For a
righteous man falls seven times yet rises up each time."[19]

According to Kabbalah, evil forces actually derive their energy by "sucking" life force from holiness. The Ultimate Leader will know how to shake off the grip of the external shells of reality and see through them to their essential kernel of holiness. Even though he may fall seven times, his essential grounding in holiness will allow him to eventually rise up, identify, and rescue holy sparks everywhere.[20]

The pattern for such a rescue operation is set in an event in the life of King David. In order to save himself, David had to feign insanity and in so doing became abhorrent to the king of Gat, who then willingly expelled him from his presence. We learn from Kabbalah that this becomes a precedent for a pattern in Jewish history—of Jews being expelled from various countries during their exile, eventually to be returned to Israel. We further find this pattern linked to a dramatic passage in the Book of Job:

> He [evil] has swallowed down riches and he shall
> vomit them up again. God shall cast them from
> his belly.[21]

Even though the Jews have been figuratively swallowed up in exile, they pray to be gathered—or in this context expelled or "vomited out" of exile—and returned to Israel with all the holy sparks that they have redeemed during their long and bitter separation from their homeland.

History has shown that when Jews become so "indigestible" that other nations cannot bear them any longer, they eventually are vomited out. The reasons are many and complex: at times the host country feels threatened by the strength of the Jews; at other times, the citizens of the host country become jealous of the Jews' material success and blame all ills on them; and most frequently, the foreign nation simply cannot stomach the Jews' stubborn attachment to their faith despite strong-arm conversion tactics that have included massacres, pogroms, and persecution of every conceivable type.[22] As the Book of Exodus relates, the Jews' slavery in Egypt, the prototype of all future exiles, began with Pharaoh saying:

> "Behold, the people of Israel are more numerous and mightier than us. Come let us deal shrewdly with them so they may not increase; otherwise in the event of war they may join our enemies in fighting against us and expel [us] from the land." So they [the Egyptians] set taskmasters over them to oppress them with forced labor...."[23]

Only after the ten plagues had devastated Egypt did the Jews finally become "indigestible," and Pharaoh expelled them.

Throughout history, the very nations that invited the Jews into their borders or forcefully brought them there, in due time came to expel them. This happened, for example, in England in 1290, in France in 1394, and in Spain in 1492—all places where Jews enjoyed significant material success. The worst case, of course, was that of Nazi Germany, and the most recent was that of the Soviet Union, which eventually found it easier to let the Jews go than to deal with the problem they posed.

After World War II, a combination of world conscience, shocked into action by the nauseating revelations of the Holocaust, and the simultaneous rise of a new proud, defiant Jew insistent on returning to his homeland, led to the rebirth of Jewish sovereignty in the land of Israel.

This phenomenon is intrinsically connected to the coming of the Messiah in that both events entail the uplifting of all the good trapped in the exile and its ultimate liberation in Israel.

At the dawning of the Messianic age, the forces of darkness and evil will attempt their final act of opposition.[24] It is not surprising, then, that in the last century, as the ingathering of the exiles began in earnest,[25] the opposite forces of genocide and assimilation have been felt with a vengeance. These forces reveal a cosmic battle of good versus evil that must occur before the Messianic era begins.

Assimilation represents the most extreme manifestation of the Jews being swallowed up while in exile, allowing a spirit of "unholy folly" not only to enter, but to overwhelm completely the Jewish spark within. Ultimately, though, no soul will be lost and eventually every spark of holiness will be brought back to Israel.[26]

In many cases a Jew, long cut off from his true roots, will begin the spiritual journey back to Judaism only after becoming totally alienated and even disgusted with the very foreign, material values he adopted at the expense of his true Jewish identity. In this sense, his own false self-identity vomits him out, thus forcing him to look deep within, where his true Jewish identity begins to reveal itself.

As is clearly evident in Israel today, the complete redemption of the sparks of holiness is neither an easy nor instantaneous process. Jews from over one hundred countries are now gathered in Israel and an intense period of self-definition and creative energy has begun. A period of recuperation from the long exile is taking place as the Jewish people heal and strengthen themselves for the last battle with the forces of evil.

As in the case of the first manifestation of the sense of folly, the process described here also follows the Ba'al Shem Tov's three stages of spiritual growth.

"Submission" in the soul is experienced in the consciousness of exile—the sensation of being swallowed up, the feeling of revulsion at false self-identity, and the spirit of "unholy folly" leading to sin.[27] Even in the land of Israel one can revert to an exile mentality. Before one is able to free oneself from the powers of darkness, a total awareness of separating good from evil and holy from profane is required. It is this stage of "separation" that most represents the second manifestation of "holy folly."[28] Only when a true separation of good and evil is accomplished can the sparks of holiness be redeemed and a "sweetening" take place where all reality is reunited with its Divine source.

## FOLLY THAT BRINGS JOY

"Holy folly" that awakens laughter and joy in others is in certain respects the simplest to understand and the easiest to access. Nonetheless, its application eludes most people. Yet, its rewards are so immediate and long lasting, it is a wonder that people find it so hard to reveal this characteristic in themselves and others.

The Talmud[29] tells us that Rabbi Shmuel ben Yitzchak used to take three branches and juggle them before a bride at a wedding. Rabbi Zeira took exception to his behavior, feeling it brought scorn upon the sages to act in such an undignified manner in public. When Rabbi Shmuel died, a pillar of fire, which only appeared once in a generation, accompanied him to his last resting place. This sign was considered an acknowledgment of his greatness from heaven. Only then did Rabbi Zeira realize how precious Rabbi Shmuel's actions had been in the eyes of God.

The ability to use humor and "a little foolishness" to cause joy and laughter in others emanates from a level of wisdom that transcends the restrictions of normative logic. When properly applied, this type of folly breaks down psychological barriers preventing people from opening up to each other and makes possible new levels of experience and consciousness. The great 3rd century sage Rabbah[30] would begin his public lectures with an amusing story or anecdote in order to relax his students and create rapport with them; in this way they would be more receptive to his teachings.

It is customary for guests at a Jewish wedding to employ a number of unusual methods to make the bride and groom laugh. The spiritual effect of such "holy folly" is to bring souls together; pure joy arouses the revelation of God's infinite light, the spiritual source of conceiving children.

Someone who dislikes this sort of folly actually prevents birth, as may be seen in the story of David and his wife Michal.[31] As the Ark of the Covenant was being brought up to Jerusalem, an event of great public celebration, King David was so overcome with joy that he began to dance wildly in the streets. Looking out of her window, Michal "despised him in her heart." When David returned to the palace, she ridiculed his behavior:

> "How glorious was the king of Israel today, who was exposed today in the eyes of the maidservants of his servants, as one of the boors would be exposed!"

But King David responded:

"It was before God Who chose me above your father, and above all his house, to appoint me prince over God's people, over Israel. Before God I will make merry. And I shall behave even more humbly than this, and I shall be lowly in my own eyes; and of the maidservants of whom you have spoken, by them shall I be held in honor."

The story concludes with the words:

And Michal the daughter of Saul had no child to the day of her death.

In the eyes of David, bringing the Ark of the Covenant to Jerusalem represented a wedding between God and Israel, worthy of "holy folly" of the highest order. Michal's disdain prevented her from reaching the level of unity of souls needed to bring children into the world.

This third type of folly differs from the two preceding categories in that they are more a means to other goals, whereas the joy evoked at this level is an end in itself.[32]

Maimonides writes concerning the joy produced by "a little foolishness" in his description of the celebrations that took place in the Temple during the week-long holiday of Sukot.[33] Every night, water would be drawn from a nearby natural spring and brought up to the Temple in a festive procession. The water would then be poured on the altar, symbolizing the people's fervent hopes for a year of abundant rain and blessing. All present would then celebrate the entire night with singing, ecstatic dancing, and acrobatics. Of these festivities the Mishnah[34] states, "He that never has seen the joy of the water-drawing celebration has never in his life seen joy."

Maimonides also notes that a commandment fulfilled with love and joy represents the spiritually purest way of serving God. He explains that if one does not serve God with joy and gladness of heart, one is worthy of punishment. He goes on to declare that anyone who feels they are too great or honorable to partake in the "holy folly" of such a *mitzvah* (as the celebration of drawing water) is, in fact, a sinner and a dunce.[35]

One of the main obstacles to reaching a state of happiness is pride, arrogance, and an inflated ego. In the same discussion Maimonides—quoting the verse from Proverbs,[36] "Do not glorify *yourself* before the king"—explains: do not put the focus on your own glory or dignity ahead of the glory due God. Anyone who holds back from engaging in an exuberant display in praise of the King of Kings out of hyper-sensitivity or self-consciousness brings honor neither to God nor to himself.

For the Jew outside the land of Israel there cannot be the same spontaneous expression of joy felt through fulfilling God's commandments as there is in the land of Israel, which is inherently conducive to experiencing the joy of a *mitzvah* as intrinsic to the *mitzvah* itself.[37] One of the major themes of the teachings of the Ba'al Shem Tov was that the time had come to experience the joy of a *mitzvah* even while in exile, as one would in the land of Israel. This change of focus—experiencing a taste of Israel while yet in exile—helped spark in the Jewish people, whether conscious or unconscious of its origin, an augmented desire to return to the land of Israel.

As with the two previous aspects of foolishness, we see once again that this type of "holy folly" follows the Ba'al Shem Tov's three stages of spiritual growth. First, one enters into a state of "submission" in order to free the ego from its inhibitions and to make space for experiencing the joy of the moment. "Separation" is accomplished by putting the self aside, so as not to detract from the pure intent of bringing happiness to others and God. Finally, after creating joy for others, one is able to experience the "sweetening"—to taste the sweetness of joy emanating from the act itself.

Within the initial "submission" there must be a hint of "sweetening" in order to motivate action, and within the level of "sweetening" there must be a hint of "submission," in order that one not get too carried away (the boundaries of joy will presently be explained). Thus is revealed the Kabbalistic notion that "the end is wedged in the beginning and the beginning in the end."

## A LITTLE FOOLISHNESS

> Death-flies stink, yet they ultimately express fragrant oil; more precious than wisdom, than honor, is a little foolishness.[38]

Reflecting once again on the words of King Solomon, which have served as our source for the concept of folly, we notice the adjective "little" modifying the word "foolishness." While this seems appropriate for the first two levels of folly we described— the folly of punishment and the folly of feigned insanity—it appears limiting in relation to the overall goal of serving God constantly with joy. Theoretically, there should be no limit to exuberance and ecstasy when approaching the service of God.

There are two ways in which we can understand the Hebrew word *me'at*, which is translated as "little" in this context: (1) downsizing the ego to be able to take joy in fulfilling God's commandments; and (2) allowing ourselves to experience a hint of ecstasy now in order to keep the goal of eventual total joy ever-present in our minds.

David's statement to Michal—"and I shall be lowly in my own eyes..."—while an explanation of his inner feelings, is actually the prerequisite for enacting all levels of spiritual service. Making one's ego small creates more space for Divine wisdom and inspiration to enter, as we have discussed. Great joy is born from the spiritual womb of "nothingness." When the ego is rectified and dedicated to serving God and making others happy, it becomes easy to partake of the joy of fulfilling a commandment.

The sages understand the words of Moses in the Book of Deuteronomy—"It is not because you are the most numerous of peoples that God chose you, for you are the fewest [*me'at*] of all people..."[39]—to teach that God chose the Jewish people because of their ability to nullify their will to His will and because of the Jews' instinctive selflessness in relation to others.[40] The "smaller" people become in their own eyes, the greater they become in the eyes of God.

A second insight relating to "a little foolishness" is a statement in the Talmud[41] that whoever recites *Hallel* every day is in fact cursing (rather than blessing). *Hallel* is an expression of ecstasy; a series of Psalms of praise and thanksgiving, it is only included in our prayers on the holidays of Passover, Shavuot, Sukot, Hanukah, and on Rosh Hodesh, the celebration of the new moon. To recite *Hallel* is to experience directly and express the festive energy of these special days; but, in the present state of consciousness, anyone who thinks he can feel the miraculous state of being in such an intense way as to justify reciting *Hallel* daily is deceiving himself.

In the Messianic age a state of consciousness will be reached in which the daily recitation of *Hallel* will be an appropriate expression of one's awareness of God's continual presence and goodness.

Although we cannot, as yet, expect to serve God unceasingly with such joyous ecstasy, it should nevertheless be a goal and the occasional recitation of *Hallel* reminds us of this. On a transcendent level, the commandments are themselves only a means to enter into an elevated state of awe—and even higher, into a state of selflessness—that reveals the joy of a commandment as its true intended purpose. The statement of the sages that "the reward of a *mitzvah* is a *mitzvah*"[42] can be understood as "the reward of a *mitzvah* is the joy born of its fulfillment."

An enigmatic statement in the Talmud[43] declares that at a certain stage in the future the commandments will become null.[44] As a candle at high noon is null to the brilliant light of the sun, the commandments in the future will exist, but will become null in comparison to the dazzling light they produce within the soul. The inner revelation of light and pure joy derived from the fulfillment of commandments—especially those performed in the spirit of "holy folly"—will reveal that action is indeed the essence of joy. When "holy folly" becomes infinitely great it will have the power to transform any positive action and produce spiritual pleasure beyond our present capacity to comprehend.

The true leader knows this, because the true leader is deeply connected to every soul, seeking to lead through example and to inspire those around him to relate to the world in a truly joyous manner. In so doing he helps uplift within himself and others the spark of the Ultimate Leader waiting to be revealed. When properly developed, this spark is transformed into the true leadership power needed by the entire world. Ultimately, every person has the responsibility to rectify his or her own spark of leadership until the individual sparks combine to create a beacon of hope in a world of spiritual darkness.

There are countless practical applications and opportunities to manifest the five dynamics of leadership in our daily lives. As idealistic and transcendent as they may seem at times, they comprise the vision that drives us towards a balanced and integrated present and, even more, a glorious future. Even the realization of but a hint of each dynamic is a step well worth taking. As the sages say:

> You are not obligated to complete the work, nor are you free to desist from it.[45]

# 7

# Conclusion

## ASCENDING INTO THE FUTURE

More than any other, the theme that connects and ultimately motivates all five dynamics of leadership is vision.

When pursuing the first dynamic, the art of compromise, one must be ever aware of the point of goodness and truth in each person, seeing beyond the dualities of this world to the vision of oneness underlying all creation. The second dynamic, the drive for wholeness and the ability to draw the supernatural into normative reality, entails a vision of a perfected future. The very nature of inspiration, the third dynamic, is aroused and invigorated by a visionary outlook on life. The preoccupation of the leader with refining the physical world and integrating all knowledge with Torah, the fourth dynamic, is predicated on the leader's perception of all existence as a unified Divine revelation. All three levels of folly, the fifth dynamic, necessitate a keen visionary awareness of the appropriate action needed at a specific moment in time.

One of the most significant contributions of the Jewish people to the world-at-large has been its ability to transmit a universal vision of redemption. Many religions, philosophies, social causes, political movements, and artistic endeavors throughout the ages have drawn their inspiration from the Torah and from the words of the Jewish prophets whose vision of a perfected world— a world of peace, love, and brotherhood—filled humanity with hope in the darkest times.

This vision is close to reality—the Messianic age is dawning. What will it bring?

According to Kabbalah, once the Messianic age begins, we can expect to experience five levels of ascending consciousness:

1) The first level will be as subtle as it will be dramatic. Subtle, because the initial revelation of the Ultimate Leader and the subsequent changes taking place at that time will all occur within the laws of nature.[1] Dramatic because the Ultimate Leader will prove his appointment as "the Anointed One," the Messiah for whom the world is waiting, by turning the hearts of all of Israel toward God and Torah; by fighting the final wars and, in so doing, establishing for eternity Jewish sovereignty in the land of Israel; by building the third Temple in Jerusalem which will be a "house of prayer for all people"[2]; by completing the ingathering of exiles; and by rectifying the entire world so that all humanity will universally recognize and worship God.

2) As the above changes occur and their effects become consciously perceived, physical reality will gradually transform and become more spiritual in its essential nature.

Maimonides explains:

> In that time there will be no hunger nor war; and no jealousy or competition. Good things will abound greatly... There will be no occupation in the world other than to know God...as it is

written, "for the earth will be filled with the knowledge of God as the waters cover the sea."[3]

When compared to our present state of reality and our far from perfect human nature, we see that what Maimonides describes as a natural development is what we now term "supernatural." This is similar to the second dynamic of leadership—the drive for wholeness—where the drive to perfection draws the future into the present, transmuting the supernatural into the natural.

3) When reality has been refined to such an extent that physical matter becomes a perfect vessel for spiritual energy, the resurrection of the dead will occur. At that stage, body and soul become completely complementary, united in harmony. Eternal life, the birthright of humanity, will triumph over the forces of entropy and death, which will cease to exist. This eventual state when eternal life will prevail is called by the sages "the World to Come."

4) The World to Come, initially manifest in the third stage, will reach its full revelation in the seventh millenium, "a time that is entirely Shabbat"—that is a day of eternal rest from physical labor. At this level, all reality will achieve a consummate state of rest and spiritual bliss. This will also be the time when each soul will receive its due reward for all the good it did in life. All that was hidden from our eyes in this world will then be revealed.

5) The last stage of spiritual and physical refinement is referred to by the sages as an era of "fifty thousand jubilees." Every seventh year in the land of Israel was the Sabbatical year, when the land rested and lay fallow, debts were annulled, and people dedicated themselves to studying the Torah. At the conclusion of seven Sabbatical cycles, the fiftieth, or "jubilee year" was celebrated. This was an additional year of rest for the land,

slaves were freed, and land reverted to its original owner. The jubilee year, like the giving of the Torah on Mt. Sinai fifty days after the exodus from Egypt, represents the culmination and completion of a Torah-cycle.

In Psalms it is stated that "a thousand years in Your eyes are as a day that has passed."[4] From a higher perspective, a millenium is a day, and so the seventh millenium of creation is its day of Shabbat, as noted above. From this same higher perspective, a year is equivalent to 365,000 terrestrial years, a jubilee to 18,250,000 years, and fifty thousand jubilees to 912,500,000,000 years!

Thus, the expression "fifty thousand jubilees" symbolizes a state of infinite revelation and elevation when even those who have achieved seemingly consummate states of righteousness and holiness will continue to ascend "from strength to strength."[5] This level of consciousness will unite the seemingly opposite state of eternal rest achieved at the previous level with continual spiritual ascent.

# THE FIFTH DIMENSION

With regard to all five ascending levels of consciousness, each previous level becomes null ("as a candle at high noon") when one rises to the succeeding level. This can be illustrated geometrically by the fact that a zero-dimensional point becomes null when incorporated within a one-dimensional line. That line, in turn, becomes null in a two-dimensional plane, which again loses its identity within a three-dimensional cube. In postulating the fourth dimension of time as being integrally bound to the three dimensions of space, Einstein posited that three-dimensional space alone is virtually null within four-dimensional space-time. *Sefer Yetzirah* speaks of yet a fifth dimension, an infinite coordinate of moral depth. Every additional dimension makes the previous state of reality appear to be null in relation to it.

A true vision of redemption depends on the ability of the individual to reveal new dimensions of spiritual attainment that until now had been hidden. However, there exists within this vision of redemption a basic existential paradox. No matter how hard we try to manifest a perfected future within an unrectified present, the fact remains that the present is not the future. The only way of reaching the future is by coming to grips with and repairing the present. Within this dilemma lies the importance of understanding vision as a process in progress, one that grows out of the present and ultimately gives birth to the future. At the same time, the vision of redemption—though ethereal and hard to always imagine—resonates as a deep truth within the soul.

In order to further understand this process it is important to grasp the intrinsic connection between vision and *hod*, the eighth of the ten *sefirot*, which exemplifies the faculty of acknowledgment in the soul.[6] One of the meanings derived from the root of the word *hod*, as noted in our introductory definition of leadership, is "thanksgiving." If one lacks a rudimentary sense of gratitude and the ability to express it, one has no viable gateway to relate to God.

These two companion meanings of *hod*—acknowledgment and thanksgiving—when applied to a vision of redemption, relate to the future and the present respectively.

By acknowledging the promise of a glorious future, even though at times it may seem incomprehensible in terms of existing reality, we help to hasten its advent. By giving thanks and being joyous in the present moment we open our hearts and minds to experience higher dimensions of future consciousness already seeded in the present.

Another meaning of the root of *hod* is "confess." In the Talmud[7] we find the expression *ten todah*, which can be translated as "give thanks" or as "confess." Confessing one's wrongdoing and relieving oneself of the burden of guilt is the first step in repentance. When the process of repentance and atonement is complete, one's natural response is indeed a deep sense of thanksgiving.

The root of the word for "wrongdoing" or "sin" (*averah*) is the same as that of the word for "past" (*avar*). On a certain spiritual level, everything done in the past—even good deeds—is wrong in relation to the present or the future if it has lulled one into complacency, into not making an attempt to improve or strive harder each succeeding day. This confirms the spiritual principle that on the ladder of life if one is not ascending, one is descending.

Rabbi Saadia Gaon,[8] a great Torah scholar and community leader in Babylonia over a thousand years ago, wrote that everyone should "repent" for yesterday, no matter how good it was, for in relation to today it is already limited. In connection with this teaching, he related the following story.

Once he visited a city and was hosted most graciously by a perfect stranger who did not know the status of his guest. Soon after Rabbi Saadia Gaon left his house, the host found out that his guest had been the great sage. He ran after him in consternation and, upon finding him, begged for forgiveness. Rabbi Saadia Gaon was quite puzzled and reassured his host that the hospitality had been truly wonderful and had lacked nothing. The host replied: "Had I known who you were, I would have treated you a thousand times better."

This incident, which had a great effect upon the sage, served in his writings as an example as to how we should grow in our consciousness of God from day to day. Our prayer to God, like the plea of the gracious host to Rabbi Saadia Gaon, should be: "Had I known You yesterday as I know You today, I would have tried a thousand times more to serve You as befits You." The sense of confession and repentance for our lack of Divine consciousness, when considered in a positive light, becomes the fuel thrusting us forward in the present towards the future.

The three meanings of *hod* enumerated above—"thanksgiving," "acknowledgment," and "confession"—relate as well to the Ba'al Shem Tov's three stages of spiritual growth: "submission, separation, and sweetening."

The response of the soul to the past—involving confession and repentance—depends on the quality of "submission." Gratitude to God for all the manifold blessings experienced in the present moment rests on one's ability to achieve "separation" of the mind and heart from the anxiety of yesterday and the uncertainty of tomorrow, feeling instead God's Presence and Divine assistance in the present moment. Acknowledging an infinitely better future represents the "sweetening" as it reveals glimpses of a changing reality even now in an unrectified world. Although the vision of redemption is but a means and a process, its reward is the experience of all future levels of spiritual attainment in some measure in the present.

The expression "coming into days"—from the verse which we examined in our discussion of the second dynamic of leadership: "And Abraham grew old, coming into days, and God blessed Abraham with all"—alludes to Abraham's ability to draw ever higher dimensions of reality into his daily life. A visionary who walks before his generation, inventing, revealing, and initiating new insights is termed "ahead of his time." He is, in fact, a bridge above time, drawing not only the future into the present but leading the past and the present into the future.

# THE WAY TO PLEASANTNESS AND PEACE

The central prayer of Judaism, the *Shema*, includes the following declaration:

> And it will be—if you vigilantly obey My commandments which I command you this day, to love God your God and serve Him with your entire hearts and with your entire souls—that I will give rain for your land in its proper time, the early rain and the late rain, and you will harvest your grain and your wine and your oil. And I will provide grass in your fields for your cattle and you will eat and be satisfied. Beware lest your hearts be swayed and you turn astray, and you worship alien gods and bow to them. And God's fury will blaze against you, and He will close off the heavens and there will be no rain and the earth will not yield its produce; and you will perish swiftly from the good land that God gives you...[9]

These words serve as a reminder that the amount of rain, and its subsequent blessings, depends ultimately on the actions of human beings. Nature and how it treats us is thus a reflection of our level of righteousness. Once the entire Jewish people return to God and His Torah, a resulting shift will occur in the balance of nature, causing it to "behave." Likewise, one of the changes to be perceived on an inner personal level at the advent of the Messianic age will be the gradual disappearance of mental and emotional friction. At present, the inner world of mind and heart vibrates mostly with static and psychic disturbance. In the future, we will begin to tune in to more and more dimensions of reality, without the accustomed static interference. People will be simply content, and this transitional time will be marked by a lack of the suffering so much identified with worldly existence.

The purification of our inner spheres will cause a corresponding change in the physical atmosphere of nature itself, eventually leading to the second level of the Messianic age when nature assumes supernatural proportions, as in the prophecy of Isaiah:

> The wolf shall dwell with the lamb, the leopard
> lie down with the kid....

This innate peace between all the elements of creation[10] relates to all peoples coming to the truth of Torah, whose ways, in the words of the Proverbs, are "ways of pleasantness and all its pathways are peace."[11]

Among the ten *sefirot*, the Divine wisdom of the Torah is synonymous with *chochmah* ("wisdom") and the supernatural. Although in this world the Torah appears to mirror reality, only when we ascend to the second level of Messianic consciousness, when physical reality begins to transform, will we become aware that the truth is quite the opposite—nature is a reflection of the Torah, which is, in the deepest sense, a blueprint for all creation.[12]

Though this is on occasion apparent within the confines of normative reality, it takes a clear mind, free of psychic disturbance, to perceive and appreciate this view.

The total metamorphosis of nature will occur at the third level—the resurrection of the dead. Nature and its inherent properties of entropy and death will be transformed and transcended by their antithesis—eternal life.[13] This phenomenon was revealed briefly to the Jews at Mt. Sinai, when all the souls left their bodies upon hearing each Divine utterance. The souls instantaneously returned through the "dew of resurrection." Their incentive to give so completely to God emanated from an intuitive understanding that the soul is in essence "a part of God above." When we reach that elevated level, we will tap into the Divine life force, the secret of the resurrection of the dead.

Although the vision of redemption is highly idealistic, it gives clarity to both the good and the seemingly less than good of the present moment. By setting a high standard, it spurs us not only to dream but to work to make our dreams come true.

# A HOUSE IN ORDER

The return of the Jews to their homeland after almost two thousand years of exile—and the subsequent rebirth of Jewish sovereignty in the State of Israel coming only a few short years after the Holocaust—has created a plethora of new opportunities as well as monumental problems for the Jewish people. Although there have been many shining examples of heroism and bravery, and even glimpses of authentic leadership during the formation and growth of the State of Israel, there is a growing awareness from all sides that classical Zionism and its vision of leadership is unprepared and inadequate to address the true challenges that face the Jewish people.

As the people of Israel grapple with their religious and cultural identity and the seemingly unresolvable political and military conflicts with their Arab neighbors, this feeling only increases.

Outside of Israel, Jewish communities are floundering as they try to deal with the staggering problems of assimilation. Bleak predictions speak of the steady erosion of Jewish population; indeed, the very existence of a Jewish Diaspora in the near future is in question.

And yet Isaiah, who formulated the first universal vision of mankind, saw the Jews as "a light unto the nations," leaving one of the most powerful images engraved on the Jewish psyche. This image has aroused the ire of many nations who resent this Divine appointment. Nevertheless, it is a reality that both the Jewish people and the world need to understand in its proper context. The subject of leadership *vis-à-vis* the Jewish people is not just an issue for the individual or a narrow, national question, but ultimately touches the very purpose and relationship of Israel to the world.

In a classic example of existential, spiritual paradox, at present, Israel must maintain its separate and unique identity in preparation for the ultimate state of unity among peoples that will prevail in the Messianic era. Furthermore, it is the mission of the Jewish people to bring the world to the stage where it will be ready for such a spiritual reality.

Such a mission is a tremendous responsibility and it requires true humility. The role of Jewish leadership ultimately emanates from an internal consciousness of submission to God's will and a concurrent awareness that one needs to put one's own house in order before looking elsewhere. It is always easier to find fault with others than to face those same personal deficiencies within oneself.

The message is clear. Before Israel can assume the type of leadership that the world so desperately needs, it must first look inward and regain its natural and authentic identity. Only then will Israel manifest itself externally on the world stage in its true and destined role, thus allowing the "lower waters" of secular knowledge and the "upper waters" of Divine wisdom to flow together, creating the cleansing waters for all mankind.

# POSTSCRIPT

Throughout this book we have encouraged the reader to apply his or her own unique qualities in order to realize leadership potential in every realm of life. Every person can see his or her own individual experience of returning to God as an example of how the whole world can do the same. Each and every redemptive act of rectification in this world thereby becomes one more stone in the pathway to the Messianic age.

The general rule regarding prophecy is that negative prophecies do not have to take place if people mend their ways, while good prophecies are guaranteed to become manifest. Though many years have passed since the prophecies quoted in this book were first voiced by the prophets, their timeliness actually increases as exile nears its end and redemption begins.

In the days to come, the Mount of God's House shall stand firm above the mountains and tower above the hills. And all the nations shall stream to it. And the many peoples shall go and say:

"Come, let us go up to the Mount of God, to the House of the God of Jacob—that He may instruct us in His ways, that we may walk in His paths."

For from Zion shall come forth Torah, the word of God from Jerusalem...[14]

# Endnotes

# Introduction

1. Isaiah 2:4, 11:6.

2. The Jewish description of the Messiah (Hebrew: *Mashiach*, from *mashach*, meaning "anoint") can best be summarized as follows: a human being, a descendant of King David—*Mashiach ben David*—who, thanks to his leadership ability and knowledge of Torah, will bring all Jews back to Israel, inspire the entire world to believe in the one God, and usher in an era of all human beings living together in peace and brotherhood.

3. See Isaiah 60:22, *Sanhedrin* 98a.

4. The Torah describes the events surrounding the giving of the Torah at Mt. Sinai. At that time, God informed the Jewish people of their role and destiny among the nations: "And now, if you listen well to My voice and observe My covenant, you shall be to Me the most beloved treasure of all peoples, for Mine is the entire world. You shall be to Me a kingdom of priests and a holy nation." (Exodus 19:5-6).

5. Isaiah 49:6.

6. *Zohar* 1:117a; *Likutei Sichot*, vol. 15, p. 42 ff.

7. The year 5600 in the Hebrew calendar—"the six-hundredth year of the sixth millennium"—corresponds to the year 1840 in the Gregorian calendar.

8. The good news is that the ascent of the "lower waters" is considered a prelude to the descent of the "upper waters" of Divine knowledge that will engulf the world and unite with the "lower waters" during the Messianic era. The great 11th century philosopher, Maimonides, ends his explanation of the awaited Messianic era with the prophecy from Isaiah (11:9): "The world will be filled with the knowledge of God like water covers the seas" (*Mishneh Torah, Melachim* 12:5).

9. [Editor's note: The following sample of events in the last month of the year 2000 dramatically illustrates the crisis in leadership worldwide: the disgraced

president of Peru, Alberto Fujimori, fled to Japan to escape charges of corruption; the prime minister of Pakistan, Nawaz Sharif, was exiled to Saudi Arabia by the army that overthrew his administration; rioting erupted in the Philippines where President Joseph Estrada faced mounting pressure to resign as an impeachment trial on the charges of corruption continued; Ukrainian president, Leonid Kuchma, was implicated in a scandal involving the gruesome murder of a journalist who had reported on charges of corruption against him; in Thailand, the front-runner in elections for prime minister, Thaksin Shinawatra, refused to withdraw his candidacy despite an indictment on charges of trying to hide $100 million in personal wealth; violence reigned in the Ivory Coast, after former Prime Minister Alassane Ouattara was denied candidacy in the elections in that country; there was rioting in Chile upon the return of former despot General Augusto Pinochet, and a decision by the courts forestalling his arrest and trial; rioting erupted in Rome, after the Pope "warmly" received the Austrian Nazi-sympathizer Joerg Haider; rioting erupted in Zimbabwe, as a consequence of a deepening economic crisis blamed on President Robert Mugabe; there was rioting in the streets of Nice, France, where the European Union met to divide up power more evenly among its members— an effort in which it did not succeed; in the United States, the election fiasco was finally decided by the courts, but the country was described as "a house divided"; in Israel, chaos reigned as the Arabs continued to riot, and Prime Minister Ehud Barak, having no support in the Knesset, resigned to force new elections.]

10. The *Haftorah* for *Shabbat Chazon* is Isaiah 1:1-27.

11. *Tamid* 32a.

12. See *Tanya* 43 (61b).

13. *Avot* 1:14.

# 1. Leadership Defined

1. The great Hassidic master, Rabbi Nachman of Breslov (1772-1810), was the great-grandson of the founder of Hassidic movement, the Ba'al Shem Tov (Rabbi Israel ben Eliezer, 1698-1760). The story as told here is abridged from Rabbi Adin Steinsaltz, *Beggars and Prayers* (New York: Basic Books, 1979), pp. 141-171. Another translation may be found in Rabbi Aryeh Kaplan's *Rabbi Nachman's Stories* (Jerusalem: Breslov Research Institute, 1983) pp. 398-410.

2. "And God planted a garden eastward in Eden; and there he put the man whom He had formed. And out of the ground made God every tree to grow that is pleasant to the sight, and good for food; the Tree of Life also in the midst of the garden, and the Tree of Knowledge of Good and Evil" (Genesis 2:8-9).

3. In fact, the sages distinguish between two phases of redemption: the "Messianic era" (*yemot hamashiach*), when the present laws of nature will still apply, and the "world to come" (*olam haba*), in which the nature of reality will be transformed.

4. In Hebrew, the term *olam haba* can be read as "the world to come," or "the world that is [now] coming" or even "the world that has [already] come."

5. Of all the teachings received from the Ba'al Shem Tov, perhaps none are as important or essential as the notion that (1) the Jewish soul "is an actual portion of God above," and (2) a spark of the Messiah is contained within each individual soul. Based on an ancient Midrashic source (*Bereishit Rabbah* 14:9), Kabbalah and Hassidism speak of five levels or gradations of the soul: the "lower soul" (*nefesh*) relates to behavior and action; the "spirit" (*ruach*) to the emotions; the "inner soul" (*neshama*) to the mind; the "living one" (*chayah*) to the bridge between the first flash of conscious insight and its superconscious origin; the "single one" (*yechidah*) to the ultimate unity of the soul in God, as manifest by pure faith, absolute devotion and the continuous readiness to sacrifice one's life for God. It is to the fifth and most sublime level of soul, the *yechidah*, that the above teachings of the Ba'al Shem Tov refer.

6. Of the ten *sefirot*—the Divine channels through which God creates and relates to the world—the following relate to speech in particular: (1) *da'at*

("knowledge"), the power to contact another soul through self-expression; (2) *binah* ("understanding"), the deep understanding of the heart that one possesses no more than what God bestows (this motivates the "service of the heart" in prayer); and (3) *chochmah* ("wisdom"), the silent sense of total selflessness conducive to becoming a receptacle for insight and inspiration that precedes speech and makes it potent. These three qualities enable the leader to establish true union with his followers, a union that is an all-inclusive state of being which reflects the supernal *keter* ("crown") above the three general levels of consciousness—*chochmah, binah,* and *da'at.*

7. 1 Kings 19:12.

8. *Sanhedrin* 8a.

9. Ecclesiastes 8:4.

10. *Tikunei Zohar,* introduction, 17a.

11. God created the world with ten utterances; these ten utterances correspond respectively to the ten *sefirot.* The concept of Divine speech as the vehicle of creation is also encapsulated in the daily morning prayers: "Blessed is the One Who spoke and the world came into being" (Daily Morning Liturgy, *Baruch She'amar*).

12. Genesis 1:27.

13. *Ibid.* 2:7.

14. *Targum Onkelos ad loc.*

15. Genesis 1:28.

16. *Bava Metzia* 58b.

17. The authoritative work compiling Torah law on this subject is *Sefer Chafetz Chaim* by Rabbi Yisrael Meir of Radin (1839-1933). See also *Malchut Yisrael,* vol. 2, *Shemirat Brit HaLashon* (p. 219 ff).

18. *Sefer Yetzirah,* "The Book of Formation," is attributed to Abraham; it was edited in the 1st-2nd century by Rabbi Akiva.

19. There are three sub-groups, composed of: (1) three "mother" letters, (2) seven "double" letters, and (3) twelve "simple" letters.

20. Genesis 29:35.

21. A Jew upon rising in the morning declares: "I am thankful [*modeh*, from the root *hod*] to You, O living and eternal King, that You returned to me my soul with mercy; great is Your faithfulness."

22. Genesis 38:26.

23. 2 Samuel 12:13.

24. The Hebrew terms for the three steps in Divine service according to the teachings of the Ba'al Shem Tov are *hachna'ah*, *havdalah*, and *hamtakah*. See *Keter Shem Tov* (ed. Kehot) 28, where the Ba'al Shem Tov himself attributes this most basic of his teachings to his own mentor, the prophet Achiyah HaShiloni.

25. In the first paragraph of the *Shema*, the cardinal declaration of God's oneness, we are instructed: "teach them [these words] to your children and speak of them when you lay down and rise up…" The sages comment: "Speak of *them*, and not of other things" (*Yoma* 14b), implying that Torah should not be a subject to be simply learned, but an all-encompassing life style to be lived, that is, all of one's words (the directing forces of one's life) should relate to Torah.

26. This is reflected in the Talmudic statement: "Even the mundane speech of the sages is Torah" (*Avodah Zarah* 19b).

27. Daniel 11:21; 1 Chronicles 29:25.

28. This power is clearly seen in the following verse: "When there is worry in a man's heart, he should suppress it, and let a good word convert it to gladness" (Proverbs 12:25). The word for "should suppress" (*yashchenah*) is interpreted by the sages to read "speak it out" (*yesichenah*)—that is, alleviate worry in the heart and sweeten it through "speaking it out." See *To Sweeten the Bitter*.

29. Zephaniah 3:9.

30. *Avot* 2:4.

31. 1 Kings 1:5.

32. Psalms 86:1.

33. See *Megilah* 31a.

34. Psalms 109:4.

35. The sages teach: "The movement of the lips is considered action" (*Sanhedrin* 65a).

36. *Berachot* 21a.

37. The numerical value of both *shefel* and *gei'ut* is 410.

38. Isaiah 63:1.

39. Ezekiel 1:4.

40. In close parallel to his concept of "submission, separation and sweetening," the Ba'al Shem Tov taught that the two stages of *chashmal* are connected by a third, intermediate level of *mal,* meaning "severance" (as in the word *milah* ["circumcision" or "cutting off"]), producing a construction of *chashmal-mal.* These two complimentary progressions correspond in the following manner: Silence (*chash*) corresponds to "submission" (*hachna'ah*); severance (*mal*) corresponds to "separation" (*havdalah*); speaking (*mal*) corresponds to "sweetening" (*hamtakah*).

41. 1 Kings 19:11-13.

42. In Kabbalah and Hassidism, the inability to express oneself represents exile, while free flowing expression represents the essence of redemption. The entire month of *Nissan* revolves around the theme of exile and redemption, slavery and freedom. These energies manifest themselves on the historic, psychological, and spiritual levels for every individual just as they have throughout the ages. The Passover *Seder* and the text of the *Haggadah,* which means "telling" and which is read on Passover night, were conceived by the sages to give full expression to the commandment to remember and speak of the deliverance of the Jews from Egypt.

43. 1 Samuel 16:1. It is further written concerning King David: "I have laid help upon one that is mighty, I have exalted one chosen out of the people. I have found David My servant..." (Psalms 89:20-21).

44. Exodus 3:10-11.

45. 1 Kings 3:7-13.

46. This is shown by the Hebrew word *chochmah,* meaning "wisdom," which when permuted spells the word *mechakeh,* meaning "wait/waiting."

47. The Ari (or the Holy Ari) is the popular name of Rabbi Yitzchak Luria (1534-1572), the most central figure of Kabbalah, whose teachings form the core of Kabbalistic doctrine and the basis for the in-depth understanding of the *Zohar.*

48. Genesis 36:31-39.

49. Significantly, only with regard to this last king is his wife mentioned, thereby alluding to the sense of inter-inclusion and the ability to share represented by the world of *tikun*.

50. 2 Samuel 23:1.

51. The idiom "a new song" (to God) appears seven times in the Bible (Isaiah 42:10; Psalms 32:3, 40:4, 96:1, 98:1, 144:9, 149:1), alluding to the uplifting of the seven emotions of the heart in new song to God with the coming of *Mashiach*.

52. Numbers 16-18.

53. Once again we see the concepts of potent speech and leadership merging as one. In Aramaic, the Hebrew word *dabar* ("speech") means "take" or "lead."

54. See *Zohar* 3:233a, 7a, 265a; *Shemot Rabbah* 3:15; *Likutei Sichot*, vol. 4, p. 1087.

55. *Sotah* 49b.

56. The Hebrew word *shaliach* ("emissary") with an additional *yud* (alluding to the essential four-letter Name of God, the Tetragramnaton, which begins with a *yud*) numerically equals *Mashiach* = 358.

57. 1 Kings 8:66.

58. The highest point of the soul, as noted earlier, is called *yechidah*.

59. Isaiah 33:17.

60. The significance of *five* dynamics relates to the five origins of speech in the oral cavity (throat, palate, tongue, teeth, and lips) from which the twenty-two letters of speech—the power of leadership—are enunciated. As mentioned above, the letter associated with the month of *Nissan*, the month of redemption is the letter *hei*, whose numerical value is five. In addition, the actual telling of the story of the Exodus, in fulfillment of the obligation to teach new generations of the liberation from Egypt, is the fifth of the fifteen rungs of the *Pesach Seder*. The story begins with the word *hei*, which in this context means "this": "this is the bread of affliction."

61. When informed that people were prophesying in the camp, Joshua burst out, "My master Moses, imprison them," but Moses replied, "Are you

jealous for my sake? Would it be that all the people of God were prophets!" (Numbers 11:29) True spiritual leaders like Moses desire more than anything else that others should achieve the same heights that they have, if not even higher. This is why Moses is compared to a candle, which can light a multitude of other candles without diminishing its own light in any way (*Midrash Tanchuma, Baha'alotecha* 12).

62. "May a new light shine on Zion and may we all soon merit to enjoy its brightness" (Morning Prayer Liturgy [general version], *Birchot Kriat Shema*).

# 2. First Dynamic

1. *Avot* 3:13. It is told that once the Ba'al Shem Tov, while sitting with his students at the concluding meal of Shabbat, quoted this saying and said no more. The simple and straightforward words penetrated into the depths of the hearts of the students. For the first time each realized that no matter how much Torah he had learned or how many commandments he had fulfilled, "if the spirit of man is not pleased with him, the spirit of God is not pleased with him."

2. Numbers 27:16-18. When Moses asked God to appoint a successor, he addressed Him as "God of the *spirits* of all flesh," that is, God who knows the character of every person. In his response to Moses, God described Joshua as "a man in whom there is *spirit*," implying that he possessed something of God's own ability to know and relate to everyone according to his true inner character.

3. *Bamidbar Rabbah* 21:5.

4. A controversy is recorded in the Talmud (*Sanhedrin* 6b) as to how judges should preferably come to a conclusion in cases of civil disagreement between people. Should they strive for strict objective judgment or compromise? The conclusion of the Talmudic debate is that whenever possible, compromise should be sought as the preferred solution to conflict. In other words, the reconciliation and peace born of compromise between two previously antagonistic parties is preferable to declaring one party totally right and the other completely wrong.

5. This signifies a worldview that dictates, "let judgment pierce the mountain" (*Sanhedrin, loc. cit.*).

6. Proverbs 3:18-17.

7. The idiom used by the sages to describe the imperative to find "objective" truth is, as noted above: "let judgment pierce the mountain." The word for "compromise" is *pesharah*, which also means "solution." To understand the idiom "let judgment pierce the mountain," it will be presently explained in the text that there are five two-syllable synonyms for "light" in Biblical Hebrew, each ending in *har*, meaning "mountain": *zohar, bohar, tohar, nohar, tzohar*. In

Kabbalah we are taught that the *tzimtzum* resulted in the disappearance of five levels of Divine light, corresponding to these five synonyms for "light." "Let judgment pierce the mountain" can thus be reinterpreted to mean: severe judgment makes an (apparent) incision in the Infinite Light, thereby creating a "vacuum," empty of God's Presence. The mentality (and experience) which follows is based upon binary logic. For the human mind to grasp that the Infinite Light is still present even in this lowest of worlds paves the way for God's ultimate oneness and light to be revealed in the world to all.

8. A connection between judgment and the experience of this world is found when the Hebrew term *olam hazeh* ("this world") is translated into Aramaic. The words in Aramaic for "this world" are *alma dein*, and by simply changing the vowel of the word *dein* to *din* it transforms the meaning to "world of judgment." The Torah actually comes to "sweeten" the initial experience of this world as a world of judgment.

At the end of *Yom Kippur*, during the final and climatic moments of prayer, the entire congregation exclaims in great emotion "*God* is God." The first Name of God (the Name *Havayah*) represents God's aspect of mercy; the second Name of God (*Elokim*) represents God's aspect of judgment. By declaring that "*God* is God," we not only recognize that the apparent opposites of mercy and judgment are in their source one, but that God ultimately "sweetens" all judgment. This realization is in fact the purpose of a leader and the Jewish people as a whole: to bring the sweetness of peace and compromise, as revealed by Torah, into the world and thereby transform it.

Without the aspect of "sweetening," the given state of the world makes the Torah seem "unrealistic." This misimpression comes from the expectation that the Torah should reflect the "reality" of the world. Yet in one of the most important Midrashic statements we learn that quite the opposite is true: "God looked into the Torah and created the world." (*Bereishit Rabbah* 1:1; *Zohar* 1:134a, 2:161a) Preceding the creation of the world, the Torah served as God's blueprint. Creation is the unfolding revelation of what appears in the Master's architectural plan. Since God has chosen to "hide" Himself in the world, giving creation an illusion of separateness so that man may have free choice, the real purpose of His Torah and His own greatness is similarly hidden.

In the account of creation, only *Elokim*, the Divine Name representing the attribute of Divine judgment, is mentioned. This Name *Elokim*—which numerically equals the Hebrew word *hateva*, meaning "nature," (86)—appears thirty-two times in the six days of creation, corresponding to the thirty-two pathways of wisdom spoken of in Kabbalah, as will be explained. Reality and nature based on Divine law and order serve to reveal the continuous influx of God's wisdom in creation, as it is written: "You have made all of them [created reality] with wisdom" (Psalms 104:24). A world of order, as manifest in the precise laws of nature, is in fact a revelation of God's goodness and love of His creation. Similarly, a leader who understands the need to discipline and teach his people is expressing his great love for them.

In its inner essence, the Torah reveals the attribute of God's loving-kindness, the polar opposite and equalizing energy of His external attribute of judgment, which is revealed more in the outer manifestation of the laws of the Torah. Compromising Torah actually only accentuates the external aspect of judgment, and thus constitutes a step backwards from the rectification of the world.

9. *Tamid* 33b.

10. Rabbi Shalom Dovber (1860-1920) was the fifth rebbe of Chabad-Lubavitch.

11. Psalms 119:12.

12. Genesis 9:27.

13. *Shabbat* 88a.

14. Exodus 24:7.

15. Maimonides is the popular name of Rabbi Moses ben Maimon (1135-1204) who is also known by the acronym formed by these words as the Rambam.

16. Similarly, it states that the Messiah will "force Israel to keep the Torah" (*Mishneh Torah, Melachim* 11:4). The Lubavitcher Rebbe, Rabbi Menachem Mendel Schneersohn, explained that the force referred to will be accompanied by "pleasantness," an apparent contradiction.

17. This happened after the miracle related in the Book of Esther, while the Jews lived under the domination of the Persian Empire; today we celebrate that miracle as the holiday of Purim.

18. When a rabbinical decree is "unrealistic," in that the majority of the generation cannot live by it, we apply the principle "let judgment pierce the mountain." The "mountain" in this case represents the decree that is suffocating the people, and must, therefore, be rescinded ("pierced"). The fact that a majority cannot live by a rabbinical decree indicates that it did not emanate from the heart of the Torah in the first place. The nullification of the decree should awaken the rabbis of the generation to seek the true golden mean within the parameters of Jewish law.

19. *Menachot* 99b. This means, as expounded by the Ba'al Shem Tov, that it is sometimes necessary to relax or take off time from the intense study of Torah in order to return refreshed to its study.

20. This situation is analogous on a personal level to a decree that the majority cannot live by, thus dictating a temporary "piercing of the mountain," or taking a step backwards to regain a more holistic perspective.

21. The three root-letters *tz-b-r* of the Hebrew word *tzibur* ("congregation") are interpreted in Hassidism to represent the entire gamut of Jewish personalities, as seen in the acronym formed by the words *tzadik* ("righteous"), *beinoni* ("in-between"), and *rasha* ("wicked"). Similar to a congregation that contains all the above components, an individual also has a "congregation" of inner powers and tendencies, some righteous and others not so righteous.

22. Regarding those with an inflated sense of pride and ego, God exclaims: "I and he cannot dwell together in the same abode" (*Sotah* 5a).

23. This is represented by the final *sefirah* of *malchut* ("kingship"), whose inner motivating force is humbleness and a genuine sense of existential lowliness.

24. *Sukah* 52a.

25. Supporting the idea that the righteous are not exempt from the ongoing process of character refinement, the *Zohar* (*cf.* 3:193b) states that Messiah will "bring the righteous to repentance." It goes without saying that all those souls on a lower spiritual level will have to repent, but what does it mean that the righteous will have to repent as well? The answer is found in the well-known statement in the Talmud: "In the place where a *ba'al teshuvah* [one who has repented and come close again to God and Torah] stands, a complete *tzadik* cannot stand" (*Yalkut Shimoni, Yeshayahu* 488). The *ba'al teshuvah*, fueled by his

many errors or "descents," has the unique ability to transmute those very mistakes, propelling him to higher levels of rectified self-consciousness and Divine awareness that even the righteous cannot reach. *Teshuvah* ("repentance") entails breaking, even for a moment, the smallest point of negative self-consciousness. The moment of *teshuvah* is so powerful that it elevates the soul to new levels of consciousness not previously attainable. It creates an enduring passion to relate to every moment as an opportunity for holiness and rectification. Inasmuch as no one is perfect, even the *tzadik* needs to break out of his own static self-conception of righteousness to ascend ever higher and closer to God.

26. After each Divine utterance, the angels brought the souls back and revived the people, until finally the people asked Moses to intercede on their behalf: "And they said to Moses, you speak with us and we will hear, but let not God speak with us or we will die" (Exodus 20:16). This is why the last eight commandments were revealed to the people by Moses. The process by which the Ten Commandments were given is similar to the above analogy of the mountain held over their heads, a dynamic of "forcing through pleasantness."

27. Ezekiel 1:14.

28. *Chagigah* 13b.

29. In summary, we see that the process of ego-rectification follows the same order as the Ba'al Shem Tov's "submission, separation, and sweetening" discussed earlier.

| 3 | Sweetening<br>*hamtakah*<br>*mal* | Purification of body and soul;<br>Torah and its commandments;<br>Unification of soul with God |
|---|---|---|
| 2 | Separation<br>*havdalah*<br>*mal* | Ego refinement;<br>Repentance;<br>Self-nullification |
| 1 | Submission<br>*hachna'ah*<br>*chash* | Relating to a broader reality;<br>Acknowledging God's goodness;<br>Performing acts of loving-kindness |

30. *Avot* 1:12.

31. See *Bamidbar Rabbah* 11:7.

32. *Ketubot* 17a.

33. Deuteronomy 16:20.

34. 1 Kings 3:16-28.

35. This is a classic example of "letting judgment pierce the mountain."

36. Malachi 2:6; Proverbs 31:26.

37. These are expressed in the *sefirot* of *gevurah* and *chesed*.

38. "He who saves one life...is as if he saves an entire universe. He who destroys one life...is as if he destroys an entire universe" (*Sanhedrin* 4:5).

# 3. Second Dynamic

1. The sages warn that one should not depend on miracles (see *Pesachim* 64b).

2. Rabbi Shmuel (1834-1882) was the fourth rebbe of Chabad-Lubavitch.

3. Esther 4:14.

4. *Ibid.* 4:16.

5. *Avot* 5:4.

6. A teaching of the Ba'al Shem Tov illustrates the intrinsic connection between spiritual and physical. On the concluding day of the *Sukot* festival, we add a new sentence to the standard *Amidah* prayer, "Who makes the wind to blow and the rain to fall." The word for "wind" (*ruach*) is also the root of the word for "spirituality" (*ruchaniut*). The word for "rain" (*geshem*) is also the root of the word for "physicality" (*gashmiut*). The Ba'al Shem Tov interpreted the above phrase as follows: After the amorphous spirituality of all the prayers and rituals of the recent holidays, it is now time to "blow away" the spiritual pleasure and bring down the actualization of our prayers into the practical life-giving "rains" of physical, daily reality. When saying "Who makes the wind blow," the Ba'al Shem Tov would make a sweeping, backhand motion, as if sending something away, and when saying "and the rain to fall," he would reach his hand high above his head, as if grasping something and then slowly draw it down to earth.

In the same way, an authentic leader is not interested only in the spiritual advancement of his followers, but is intimately concerned with their earthly needs and predicaments as well. This concern stems from his understanding that physical reality is intrinsically holy and inseparable from a healthy spiritual outlook on life.

7. *Megliah* 14a.

8. When the prophet Elisha promised the Shunemite woman a child, (as related in 2 Kings 4:8 ff), he said: "Next year at this time, you shall embrace a son." The woman, aware that the angel who had promised a child to Sarah had said that he would return the following year, suspected that Elisha—who did

not say that he would return—was not willing to commit himself to verifying his promise. He calmed her by saying that "the angel who lives forever was able to say 'I will return in a year's time,' but I am just mortal flesh and blood. Whether I am alive or not, in a year's time, you shall embrace a son" (commentary of Rashi [Rabbi Shlomo ben Yitzchak, 1040-1105], the French Biblical and Talmudic commentator, on Genesis 18:10).

In other words, Elisha was telling the woman that his prophecy concerning her was not dependent upon himself but coming directly from God. Although this reinforces the miraculous nature of the prophecy, it also paradoxically makes it less "spectacular" (as a unique act of an individual) and more "natural" (for who is more natural to creation than God the Creator Himself?).

9. Numbers 11:29.

10. This is known as *mesirut nefesh*, literally, "offering of the soul."

11. *Keter Shem Tov* (ed. Kehot) addendum 116.

12. In the Kabbalah, the 600,000 male souls of Israel over the age of 20 that left Egypt and received the Torah are seen as representing the archetypes of all Jewish souls, past, present, and future. From the verse, "and the children of Israel went out of Egypt in their fifth" (Exodus 13:18), we learn that each of these archetypal souls belongs to a group of five related souls, including the women and children of each one's immediate family. This brings the total number of Jews who left Egypt to 3,000,000.

A *minyan* is the quorum of ten men required for Jewish communal prayer. Ten is the first number whose total number of permutations ($10! = 10 \cdot 9 \cdot 8 \cdot \ldots \cdot 2 \cdot 1 = 3,628,800$) exceeds 600,000 as well as 3,000,000 (see *The Hebrew Letters*, p. 164). In Kabbalah, we are taught that every permutation of a group of souls (every unique order of the souls, one following the other) is itself a manifestation of an individual soul. Thus, every quorum of Jews reflects the presence of the entire Jewish people: men, women, and children. This collective presence is the "sanctuary" in which God's Presence dwells.

13. See Rashi on Deuteronomy 29:28. Before advancing toward the Promised Land, the Jews took a vow to be faithful to the statutes of the Torah in the Holy Land and become responsible for one another.

14. Joshua, chapters 1-6.

15. *Ibid.*, chapter 7. As an outgrowth of these events, the Talmud teaches that no person is an island, each is responsible for the actions of others as well as his or her own, because each exists as part of the whole (*Shavuot* 39a).

16. Isaiah 2:3.

17. *Degel Machaneh Ephraim, V'etchanan, s.v. V'etchanan.*

18. Isaiah 49:10.

19. The importance of the attribute of compassion is seen in the Kabbalistic model of the *sefirot*. Each of the ten *sefirot* is associated with a particular Name of God. The four-letter essential Name of God, the Tetragrammaton, is associated with *tiferet* ("beauty"), whose inner motivational force is compassion. As representatives of God, we must attempt to manifest this quality as much as possible in our daily lives. Through giving and consciously sweetening reality we create moments of rectification, islands of Divine perfection in a sea of human sorrow.

20. *Shemot Rabbah* 2:2.

21. *Chagigah* 13a.

22. Proverbs 12:25.

23. See *To Sweeten the Bitter.*

24. The numerical value of the above phrase "worry in the heart of man" in Hebrew (*da'agah b'lev ish*) equals the numerical value of the word *Mashiach* (358). Neither the Messiah's own personal anxiety nor mankind's will be relieved until he redeems the world from its suffering and unites God and man, thus bringing a sense of wholeness and completeness to all of reality.

25. The soul of Zevulun comes from *keter* ("crown"), the highest of *sefirot*, while the soul of Issachar emanates from the next *sefirah, chochmah* ("wisdom"). The root of the Hebrew word for "business" (*sechorah*)—the realm of Zevulun and the model sphere most symbolizing materialism—in Aramaic means "surround" (*sechor*). *Keter* represents the concept of God "surrounding/transcending all worlds," whereas *chochmah* represents the idea of God "filling/permeating all worlds."

26. In the Torah account of creation we read: "To the man He said, 'Because you listened to your wife, and ate from the tree which I commanded you, saying, "Do not eat from it," the soil will be cursed because of you. In

sorrow you shall eat from it all the days of your life. It will grow thorns and thistles for you and you will eat the herbs of the field. By the sweat of your brow you will eat bread, until you return to the ground for from it were you taken. For you are dust and to dust you shall return'" (Genesis 3:17-19).

27. This is also related to the blessing of Jacob, which placed the merchant ahead of the scholar.

28. This impression is called the *reshimu.*

29. The juxtaposition and primordial order of vessels and lights is reflected in the relationship between the Jewish people, the land of Israel, and the vessels in the Temple. When the Jewish people entered the land of Israel at the time of Joshua they came from the south. According to tradition, *Mashiach* will enter Israel from the north, from where most of the exiles will return as well. It is taught in the Talmud that "he who seeks wisdom should turn to the south, he who seeks riches should turn to the north" (*Bava Batra* 25b). During their forty-year sojourn in the desert the Jewish people were surrounded by the miraculous, experiencing an insulated spiritual existence. Thus, reflecting this frame of mind, they came into the land from the south. *Mashiach,* on the other hand, will enter from the north, symbolizing the dependence of the future redemption on the rectification of the physical world and its becoming a proper vessel for the spiritual.

In the Tabernacle in the desert and later in the Temple, twelve loaves of bread—symbolizing material sustenance—were placed on a golden table situated on the north side. On the south side was the *menorah,* the seven-branched candelabrum, the symbol of light and spirituality.

In the Mishnah (*Avot* 4:13) we are taught that there are three crowns: the "crown of royalty" (*keter malchut*), the "crown of Torah" (*keter Torah*), and the "crown of priesthood" (*keter kehunah*). These three crowns form three pillars of leadership, both political and spiritual. When describing the construction of the vessels in the Tabernacle, the Torah prescribes that the table upon which the bread rested, the holy ark, and the golden incense altar all should be constructed with a golden lattice crown surrounding the top of the base. These crowns correspond to the three crowns of leadership as described in the Mishnah in the following manner:

| Ark | *Keter Torah* | Crown of Torah |
| Golden altar | *Keter kehunah* | Crown of priesthood |
| Table of shewbread | *Keter malchut* | Crown of kingship |

The power invested in the crown of Torah emanates from the tablets of the law kept in the ark. This energy is then drawn to the golden altar and the crown of priesthood by way of the candelabrum, the symbol of light and spirituality. This progression is alluded to in the words for "ark" (*aron*) and "candelabrum" (*menorah*): both words contain the letters composing the word for "candle" (*ner*), a source of light. In Kabbalah we are taught that the crown of kingship (unlike the two connected crowns of priesthood and Torah, symbolizing light and spirituality) is an independent energy in its own right. The connection between kingship and the bread alludes to a king's responsibility to provide society with the proper economic structure enabling the physical needs of the nation to be secured. The rectification of the physical as a prerequisite to the rectification of the spiritual is reflected in the saying of the sages: "If there is no flour there is no Torah" (*Avot* 3:17).

The surrounding golden crowns on three of the cardinal components of the Tabernacle reveal the very purpose of the Temple—to be a finite, physical space where the infinite, eternal Divine Presence of God can "dwell," a meeting point between God and man. The word used in the Torah for each of these "crowns" (*zer*) also means "strange" (*zar*), a meaning that alludes to the surprising secret in Kabbalah that the source of the vessels is higher than the source of the lights. When the letters of the word for "crown" (*zer*) are inverted they form the word for "secret" (*raz*).

In the continuation of the above teaching in the Mishnah, we are taught that there is one more crown above the others—the crown of a good Name. The Ba'al Shem Tov, "the Master of the Good Name," made the need to unite physical and spiritual a centerpiece of his teachings, as well as his actions. Hassidic thought comes to reveal the deepest secrets of Kabbalah and integrate them into people's daily lives. It was by design that the Ba'al Shem Tov devoted himself to the so-called simple, common people—whom he saw to be innately connected to the very essence of God—for it was they who could appreciate the depths and essence of his teaching often to an even greater extent than the more intellectual elite. The Ba'al Shem Tov succeeded in bringing the intellectual elite to become inspired to serve God sincerely by observing the pure, unadulterated Divine service of the simple Jew.

The "Good Name" of which the Ba'al Shem Tov was "Master" is the Name of God that is spelled *alef-hei-vav-hei*, whose numerical value is the same as that of the Hebrew word *tov*, meaning "good" (17). According to Kabbalah, as with regard to the essential four-letter Name of God, the Tetragrammaton, the first two letters of this Name correspond to spiritual and intellectual forces, whereas the second two letters correspond to the more physical aspects of emotion and action. The "Master of the Good Name" knows how to unite these two pairs of letters in perfect harmony, bringing wholeness and completeness to the world.

30. Genesis 24:1.

31. Isaiah 11:9.

# 4. Third Dynamic

1. *Avot* 4:3.

2. The source of leadership, the *sefirah* of *malchut*, is specifically in the "unknowable head" (*reisha d'lo ityada*) above all other powers of the soul. It is the highest point of the three heads of the supernal *sefirah* of *keter* ("crown").

3. As it is written, "the [true] servant of a king is himself like a king" (*Shavuot* 47b).

4. In the Hassidic model of leadership, the leader-to-be first begins preparing himself by delving into the inner dimensions of Torah. When he begins to teach these mysteries to his students, it awakens in them the desire to return to closeness with God, which is indeed the teacher's primary intention. The response of his students to his teachings arouses in him a certain level of awareness of his leadership potential, which he begins to actualize by first creating a network to efficiently disseminate his teachings to wider circles. Though his efforts are now directed publicly, at this stage only a small part of his potential is recognized by himself and others.

5. Isaiah 49:10. Our sages, noting the use of the future tense of the verb "*will* lead them" in this verse, comment: "Any leader who leads the community pleasantly [i.e., with compassion] will merit to lead them in the [Messianic] future" (*Sanhedrin* 92a).

6. The Ba'al Shem Tov taught that the three general dimensions of reality are: Worlds, Souls, and Divinity. In accordance with the general principle of inter-inclusion, each of these general categories possesses within itself all three as sub-categories. As the attribute of compassion relates essentially to Souls (one soul feels compassion for another, suffering soul), we may see the three levels of compassion described here as corresponding to the inter-inclusion of Worlds within Souls, Souls within Souls, and Divinity within Souls.

Our sages teach us that each individual soul is an entire "world" in its own right (*Sanhedrin* 37a). The descent of the soul from the higher worlds to this lowest world is further an image of Worlds. The compassion towards the "fallen" individual soul is thus at the level of Worlds within Souls.

The Ba'al Shem Tov taught that the essence of the level of Souls is the loving connection and interrelation of all Jewish souls. Here, one's consciousness is directed to the people of Israel as a whole. One identifies with the struggle of the people throughout the ages, living Jewish history and feeling immense compassion for the plight of the Jewish people. This is the level of Souls within Souls.

The Divine Presence itself, the *Shechinah*, is referred to in Kabbalah as "the congregation of Israel" (*Kenesset Yisrael*). It is the ultimate source of the Jewish people as a whole, "accompanying," as it were, the people throughout history and especially in exile, as our sages say: "the Divine Presence went into the exile of Babylonia with them; the Divine Presence went into the exile of Edom with them" (*Megilah* 29a).

Compassion for the *Shechinah* in exile is thus at the level of Divinity within Souls.

To summarize:

| 3 | Divinity within Souls | Compassion for the *Shechinah* in exile |
|---|---|---|
| 2 | Souls within Souls | Compassion for the Jewish people in exile |
| 1 | Worlds within Souls | Compassion for the individual soul in exile |

7. In the terminology of the Ba'al Shem Tov employed in the footnote above, the experience of compassion is at the general level of Souls, but what it elicits—Divine inspiration (to redeem the exiled level of Souls)—descends from the general level of Divinity. In particular, compassion at the level of Worlds within Souls arouses inspiration to descend from the level of Worlds within Divinity; compassion at the level of Souls within Souls arouses inspiration to descend from the level of Souls within Divinity; and compassion at the level of Divinity within Souls arouses inspiration to descend from the level of Divinity within Divinity.

| | Level of compassion | Inspiration elicited |
|---|---|---|
| 3 | Divinity within Souls | Divinity within Divinity |
| 2 | Souls within Souls | Souls within Divinity |
| 1 | Worlds within Souls | Worlds within Divinity |

8. Deuteronomy 13:18.

9. "He is the first redeemer; he is the last redeemer" (see *Shemot Rabbah* 4:2; *Zohar* 1:253a). The intimate connection between inspiration and compassion is similar to the intrinsic connection between compassion and selflessness, the two qualities linking the two manifestations of this great soul.

10. Numbers 12:3.

11. Exodus 16:6-8.

12. The *sefirah* of *chochmah* and its inner power of selflessness is connected to *tiferet* and its inner power of compassion, as alluded to in the following verse: "What is his name and what is his son's name" (Proverbs 30:4). In Kabbalah, *chochmah* always refers to "father" and *tiferet* to "son." Referring back to the statement "He is the first redeemer; he is the last redeemer," we infer from this that Moses is the "father" and *Mashiach* the "son." A numerical Torah gem reveals that "Moses" (*Moshe*, 345) equals the sum of the Hebrew words for "selflessness" (*bitul*, 47) and "compassion" (*rachamim*, 298). A further numerical support for the connection between *bitul* and *rachamim* is found in the above-quoted verse, "And He will give you compassion and have compassion on you." The numerical value of this verse equals the sum of all the numbers from 1 to 47 (1128). Here we see that true and complete compassion gives rise to selflessness. This is because the source of compassion, the inner quality of the *sefirah* of *tiferet*, is in the super-conscious *sefirah* of *keter*, the ultimate soul-root of *Mashiach*.

From this we learn an important lesson: the one best able to exhibit compassion is the one with the greatest sense of *bitul*. Another allusion to the connection between these two qualities is contained in the first two letters of the Torah, *beit* and *reish* (of the word *bereishit*, "in the beginning"). The letter *beit* is the initial letter of the word *bitul*, and the letter *reish* is the initial letter of the word *rachamim*.

Self-nullification of will in relation to God and man is manifest on two distinct levels. In relation to God, one's own will is nullified in order to do God's will, as revealed in the study of Torah and the performance of *mitzvot*. This idea is best expressed in the Mishnah (*Avot* 2:4): "Make His will as if it was your will in order that He may make your will as if it was His will." In relation to man, one must be sure that any action initiated for the sake of others comes from sincere intent and not from self-serving interests or hidden agendas.

13. See *Igeret HaKodesh* 8; also see *Bava Batra* 10a.

14. Genesis 29:1-11.

15. Rabbi Shneur Zalman of Liadi (1745-1812), the first Rebbe of Chabad-Lubavitch, authored the *Tanya*, the seminal work of Chabad Hassidism.

16. In this citation as well, the words for "kiss you" (*eshakcha*) and "give you to drink" (*ashkecha*) are spelled identically; only the vowels differ.

17. Song of Songs 8:1-2.

18. Exodus 14:15.

19. Genesis, Chapters 32-33.

20. The Aramaic word for "prayer" normally used in the Talmud is *rachamei*, coming from the same root as the Hebrew word *rachamim*, meaning "compassion." This illustrates the intimate connection between compassion and inspiration. We are taught in Kabbalah and Hassidism that the chief weapon of *Mashiach* is his prayer, which derives from his consummate sense of compassion.

21. Isaiah 11:2-3.

22. On Passover, Shavuot, and Sukot, the three pilgrimage holidays of the year, it is customary when taking the Torah out of the ark for its public reading, to recite a special prayer which contains the request: "Privilege us that You may rest Your Presence upon us and radiate upon us a spirit of wisdom and insight. Let there be fulfilled in us the verse that is written: 'The spirit of God shall rest upon him, the spirit of wisdom and understanding, the spirit of counsel and might, the spirit of knowledge and fear of God.'"

23. According to tradition, the four senses of sight, hearing, taste, and touch were all blemished due to their participation in the sin of eating from the Tree of Knowledge of Good and Evil in the Garden of Eden. Only the sense of

smell does not appear in the verses describing the first sin, implying that, not having been blemished, it has retained its original pristine state.

24. Isaiah 11:9.

25. Each of the four levels of inspiration in the citation of Isaiah is referred to as "a spirit." In Hebrew, the word for "spirit" (*ruach*) also means "direction." The four "spirits" of the Ultimate Leader thus allude to the four directions of the world. Until the coming of the Messiah, our sages teach us, the fourth direction (from which evil enters the world) remains open, and only he will be able to close it. This implies that only he will be able truly to achieve the fourth "spirit"—"the spirit of knowledge and fear of God."

26. Rashi explains: "It is pleasing (*nachat ruach*) to Me that I have spoken and My will has been done" (*Sifrei, Shelach* 1, *et al.*).

27. Genesis 8:20-21.

28. *Ibid.* 5:28-29.

29. Rashi on Genesis 5:29.

30. The "spirit of God" initially manifests itself as inspiration. Thereafter it descends and encompasses the other three levels of "spirit." Ultimately, the inspiration is fully integrated, coming to a state of rest "as waters cover the sea." The revelation of inspiration and its eventual state of rest is alluded to in the two juxtaposed appearances of the name Noah in the first verse of the Torah portion named for him: "These are the generations of Noah. Noah was a righteous man, perfect in his generation ..." (Genesis 6:9).

31. The expression "the day which will be completely Shabbat and a rest day for eternal life" is taken from *Tamid* 7:4.

32. Genesis 6:7.

33. *Zohar* (*Hashmatot*) 1:254b.

34. Genesis 18:17-18.

35. There were five cities in total about to be destroyed (though they are referred to collectively as "the city"). Abraham asked initially that destruction be forestalled if fifty righteous men could be found—ten for each city (*Targum Yonatan* to Genesis 18:17).

36. Genesis 18:26-29.

37. According to the Ari.

38. Exodus 32:9-10.

39. *Ibid.* 32:14.

40. *Ibid.* 32:31-32.

41. *Zohar* 1:106a.

42. *Vayikra Rabbah* 29:11.

43. Genesis 5:24.

44. The numerical value of the last two letters of Chanoch equals that of God's Name, the Tetragrammaton (26), thus alluding to the verse: "And Noah found grace (*chen*) in the eyes of God."

45. As follows: (1) Adam, (2) Seth, (3) Enosh, (4) Keinan, (5) Mahalalel, (6) Yered, (7) Chanoch, (8) Methuselah, (9) Lemech, (10) Noah, (11) Shem, (12) Arpachshad, (13) Shelach, (14) Ever, (15) Peleg, (16) Re'u, (17) Serug, (18) Nachor, (19) Terach, (20) Abraham, (21) Isaac, (22) Jacob, (23) Levi, (24) Kehat, (25) Amram, (26) Moses.

46. Deuteronomy 34:5-7.

47. Moses' mission had been completed in that incarnation. The soul of Moses returns in every generation to continue its work to rectify all the souls of Israel (including those of the mixed multitude that he accepted into the fold of Israel at the time of the Exodus) by revealing more and more of the wisdom of the Torah, thus preparing us for the final redemption which will be ushered in by the Messiah.

48. We will discuss in detail the Seven Noahide Commandments in our examination of the Fourth Dynamic of Leadership.

49. "In the six-hundredth year of Noah's life, in the second month, on the seventeenth day of the month, on that day, all the fountains of the great deep burst forth and the windows of heaven were opened. And the rain was upon the earth forty days and forty nights" (Genesis 7:11-12).

The *Zohar* interprets the above verse prophetically by stating that in the six-hundredth year of the sixth millennium the wellsprings of lower wisdom will open below and the gates of higher wisdom will open above in order to prepare the world for the Messianic redemption and the seventh millennium of eternal rest. The macro cycle of six thousand years followed by a seventh millennium of the World to Come corresponds to the micro cycle of six days of labor and a seventh day of rest.

As noted earlier, the year the *Zohar* mentions as the year when the floodgates of knowledge will open—5600 in the Hebrew calendar—corresponds to the year 1840 in the Gregorian calendar. This year approximates the beginning of the industrial revolution and great leaps forward in the physical sciences.

The lower springs of wisdom represent the totality of all technological, industrial, and scientific progress (as well as progress in the social sciences and arts) made in recent times, which, when elevated to its spiritual source will serve as the foundation for the Messianic era.

The *Zohar* compares this process of the physical paving the way for the spiritual to the intense preparations for Shabbat that occur every sixth day. Only by virtue of these efforts do we fully appreciate the seventh day of rest. The idea of a cycle of exertion followed by a period of rest is inherent in the universe and relates to the dictates of physics that all energy seeks to descend to its lowest energy level, that is, its essential state of "rest."

The spiritual and physical laws just mentioned are reflected in the enigmatic statement in the Midrash that the initial arousal and ultimate purpose of creation was that "God desired a dwelling in the lower worlds" (*Tanchuma*, *Naso* 16).

This state of complete rest as the purpose of creation clarifies an even deeper, yet unfulfilled, meaning of the name *Noah*, "rest." We discussed above how inspiration is transformed into compassion and compassion demands taking action. Although Noah failed to fully translate inspiration into action, he was successful in certain respects. His all-consummate sense of rest, as manifest in his passivity in pleading for his generation, unfolded too soon before the flood, as well as afterwards, when he succumbed to a drunken stupor. Noah, nonetheless, remains a prototype of future leaders, each one developing and rectifying his initial, immature spark that is the spark of the Ultimate Leader.

50. The forty days of rain symbolize the minimum measurement of forty *seah* of water needed for a kosher *mikveh*, the ritual pool used for spiritual purification. In conceptual terms, the world was submerged in a *mikveh* to purify it from the gross level of spiritual impurity to which it had sunk.

51. The Talmud states that Bezalel—the chief artisan of the Tabernacle, the portable "Temple" of the desert generation—was so wise that he "knew how to permute the letters through which heavens and earth were created" (*Berachot* 55a).

52. The inner motivating force of the *sefirah* of *chochmah* ("wisdom") is selflessness, the opposite of intellectual pride and prowess, as it is written: "When pride comes, then comes shame; but with modesty comes wisdom" (Proverbs 11:2). As noted earlier, the letters of the word for "I" (*ani*) permute to form the word for "nothing" (*ayin*). The imagery of Noah hidden in the ark until the flood subsided exemplifies both the wisdom to wait as well as the consciousness of being "nothing" in relation to God.

53. See *Keter Shem Tov* (ed. Kehot) addenda 7, 8.

54. The Ba'al Shem Tov further explained that the three floors of the ark represent three levels of human consciousness mentioned above: Worlds, Souls, and Divinity. The level of Worlds implies the experience of reality, whether physical or spiritual, as we perceive it. The level of Souls implies the sense of creative consciousness wherein we interact with creation. The level of Divinity implies the one, true reality behind the multiplicity of creation.

55. Whereas wisdom connotes the lightning flash of intuitive inspiration, understanding infers the ability to nurture to birth the seed of pure thought. For this reason wisdom and understanding are referred to in Kabbalah as "two companions who never separate" (see *Zohar* 3:4a).

56. This idea is encapsulated in the famous letter of the Ba'al Shem Tov to Rabbi Gershom of Kitov: "... I ascended from level to level until I entered the chamber of the *Mashiach*.... I asked the *Mashiach*: 'when will the Master come?' And he answered: 'By this you shall know: When your teachings become public and revealed in the world, and your wellsprings burst out to the farthest extremes...'"

57. Exodus 24:7.

58. *Kidushin* 40b.

59. *Ibid.*

60. Maimonides in his classic description of the Messianic era states that the *Mashiach* will begin his career by teaching the (Oral) Torah, educating the people to abide by its precepts. The oral tradition of the Torah includes the

wisdom of Kabbalah. Hassidism teaches that only through understanding the inner wisdom of the Torah can the Written and Oral Torah be truly united.

Due to the enormous changes in the world in the last 250 years, it sometimes appears that the figures and heroes of the Bible are of a completely different mindset than we are today, or even than were the teachers of the period of the *Mishnah* and *Gemorah*. Even in the scholarly world of the *yeshivah*, the great emphasis has been on studying the Oral Torah (the Talmud and Jewish law) somewhat at the expense of in-depth study of the Written Torah (the Bible: the Five Books of Moses [often referred to alone as "Torah"], the Prophets, and the Writings). It is only through studying the secrets of the Torah that we come to understand the mentalities of the Written and Oral Torah as being the same. The farther away we get from Sinai, the more necessary it is to learn the inner secrets of Torah to bridge the growing gap of time. The farther we are from Sinai, the closer we are to the *Mashiach*, the one who will inspire all of Israel, and eventually the entire world, with the secrets of Torah and the revealed "spirit of wisdom and understanding."

61. Genesis 8:17.

62. The "spirit of God," when bestowed upon various judges and prophets in the Bible, is sometimes translated in the *Targum* as the "spirit of prophecy" and at other times as the "spirit of might." The "spirit of prophecy" refers to the "spirit of wisdom and understanding," while the "spirit of might" naturally relates to the "spirit of counsel and might."

63. "Be fruitful and multiply and fill the land. The fear of you and the dread of you shall be upon every beast of the earth...into your hand are they given" (Genesis 9:1-2). The fear that the animal kingdom conjured up in man was to be a thing of the past, a pre-flood reality that, along with man's other fears, could now be different.

64. Genesis 9:11.

65. *Ibid.* 11:4.

66. *Ibid.* 11:8.

67. Both of these levels are alluded to in God's Thirteen Attributes of Mercy, which were revealed to Moses in response to the great compassion he showed for his generation after the sin of the golden calf. The essential, four-

letter Name of God, the Tetragrammaton, which is associated with compassion, appears twice before the listing of the thirteen attributes:

> And God passed by before him, and proclaimed, "*God, God, God, [Havayah, Havayah, Kel]* merciful and gracious, long suffering, and abundant in goodness and truth, keeping mercy for thousands, forgiving iniquity and transgression and sin, and that will by no means clear the guilty; visiting the iniquity of the fathers upon the children, and upon the children's children, to the third and to the fourth generation" (Exodus 34:6-7).

According to tradition there is a vertical line separating these two Names. It is explained in Kabbalah and Hassidism that the first Name represents the pre-creation, transcendent essence of God, whereas the second Name represents the post-creation, immanent aspect of God that recreates the world at every moment. The line symbolizes the *tzimtzum*, the primordial contraction needed to create "space" for a reality "outside" of God, as it were. All wisdom and understanding derives from the Name of God after the contraction. Following *Mashiach*, the inspiration we will receive through action will come directly from the transcendent, pre-creation aspect of God.

This level of inspiration is represented by the phrase in the Friday night *Shabbat* prayer *Lecha Dodi*: "the end of action is first in thought," reflecting the initial arousal within the consciousness of God, as it were, to create the world. The consummate level of "we will do and we will hear," revealed and experienced by the people at Sinai, will be fully manifest only in the Messianic era.

68. "For to us a child is born, to us a son is given; and the responsibility is upon his shoulder; and his name shall be called 'Wondrous counselor [of] the mighty God, the everlasting Father, the Prince of peace'" (Isaiah 9:5).

According to certain commentaries, the first three appellations in this verse refer to God Himself, who calls *Mashiach* "prince of peace." According to these authorities, the verse should be read: "...and his name shall be called [by] the wondrous Counselor, the mighty God, the everlasting Father: 'the prince of peace.'" But even according to this reading, it is clear that those unique attributes that are used to characterize God in the context of calling *Mashiach* by name are reflected in the soul of *Mashiach* himself.

69. Isaiah 25:1.

70. Before his appointment, the Ultimate Leader—due to his elevated sense of selflessness—will draw insight and wisdom from the continually flowing spring of Divine inspiration accessible to him from the lower, immanent aspect of God's light. This level is like that of the patriarchs and matriarchs, who are called the "Divine chariot" (*Bereishit Rabbah* 47:6). It is stated in the Talmud that even before Sinai the patriarchs observed all the laws of the Torah (*Midrash Tanchuma, Behar* 1), but before Sinai, they metaphorically only "smelled" the fragrance of the precious oil of the *mitzvot* (*Shir HaShirim Rabbah* 1).

Now, after the giving of the Torah, we possess, in performance of the *mitzvot*, the oil itself. But, as all is relative, the Torah and *mitzvot* of our time (in which the essence of the act of the *mitzvah* is not revealed) are mere "fragrance" in comparison to the revelation of Divine light in every *mitzvah* with the coming of *Mashiach*. After *Mashiach*, our level of performing *mitzvot* will be on the level of "the act [itself] is great," analogous to the revelation of the very essence of the precious oil itself. The performance of *mitzvot* at present will seem to be only like "smelling" in comparison to that future revelation.

One of the major differences between fulfilling *mitzvot* at present and in the time to come is that no one now, including the greatest of *tzaddikim*, can act totally free of ulterior considerations, even if the motive is for the best of intentions. In this sense, the concept of "the act" has to be liberated from any earthly dependency and redeemed by being elevated to the state of a pure "*mitzvah* [performed] according to Your will."

When we transcend the level of ego motivation and relate to the world by being "one handbreadth above the earth," all our thoughts, speech and actions will be elevated and become "wondrous."

71. As in "I will teach you wisdom" (Job 33:33).

72. *Avot* 5:25.

73. *Rosh HaShanah* 21b. The "fifty gates of understanding" are the fifty levels of knowing the oneness of God in His creation and ultimately; the fiftieth gate, knowing God Himself.

74. *Berachot* 4a.

75. Leviticus 23:15-16.
76. Isaiah 64:3.

# 5. Fourth Dynamic

1. Genesis, chapter 10.

2. As alluded to in the name *Israel* being read *li rosh*, "I have a head," when the letters are permuted.

3. In general, we are taught that the mind rules the heart, but it is also taught that the inner point or dimension of the heart rules the mind (see *The Mystery of Marriage*, p. 201).

4. *The Kuzari*, a philosphical work describing a disputation conducted before the King of the Khazars by a Jew, a Christian, a Muslim, and an Aristotelian philosopher, was written by Rabbi Judah ha-Levi (1075-1141).

5. At times, even a slave can elevate himself to being a faithful servant and imagine the pleasure of the master, but he cannot reach the level of the child of the master. The highest level is reached when the characteristics of child and faithful servant are unified, giving boundless pleasure to the individual as well as to God, the Master of the Universe.

6. Exodus 19:6.

7. Launching his public education campaign in 1983, the Lubavitcher Rebbe, Rabbi Menachem Mendel Schneersohn, declared that the time was ripe to begin teaching the seven Noahide commandments. As a result of his efforts, the U.S. Congress passed a bill proclaiming the universal relevance of the seven Noahide commandments.

8. Numbers 23:9.

9. Leviticus 25:35.

10. *Mishneh Torah, Yesodei HaTorah* 2:2.

11. *Avot* 5:26.

12. In the Midrash (*Eichah Rabbah* 2:13) we are taught that if one is told there is wisdom among the nations he should believe it, but if told there is Torah among the nations he should not believe it. Torah is not merely an intellectual pursuit whose goal is human or even Divine wisdom. Rather it is an

all-encompassing lifestyle whose true wisdom is imparted only to those who fully live according to its instruction.

The Talmudic statement asserts that we should believe there is wisdom among the nations. An alternative way of interpreting the statement is: There *is* wisdom among the nations, and it should be brought under the "wings of faith" by illuminating it with the light of the Torah.

13. Before secular wisdom can be totally integrated with a spiritual Torah consciousness, it needs to be refined and uplifted. This process also follows the three-stage process of "submission, separation, and sweetening":

> (1) "Submission": A Jew must humble himself to accept that wisdom is coming, at first appearances, from a non-Torah source; simultaneously, the particular body of wisdom submits itself to scrutiny, so to speak, in order to be returned to its ultimate Divine source.

> (2) "Separation": Following an initial process of refinement, the secular shells surrounding the pure kernel of wisdom are separated from it, thus exposing its natural connection to Torah.

> (3) "Sweetening": Ultimately, the essential truth is united with the Divine wisdom of the Torah, leading to the cross-fertilization of ideas between them and thereby to the final rectification.

14. Ecclesiastes 3:20.

15. It is important to note that while scientific theories may come and go, each reflects some human insight which further reflects some ultimate truth (though possibly manifest in another form altogether).

16. *Bereishit Rabbah* 12:11.

17. "The supernal crown is the crown of *malchut*" (*Tikunei Zohar*, introduction [17a]).

18. Genesis 2:5.

19. *ad loc.* Rashi is an acronym and the popular name of Rabbi Shlomo Ben Yitzchak (1040-1105) who was the French Biblical and Talmudic commentator.

20. According to tradition (*Vayikra Rabbah* 18:1), when a body is buried in the earth it completely disintegrates except for a small bone connecting the neck with the spinal column, called the *luz* bone. This bone is considered indestructible and remains in the earth until the time of the resurrection of the dead, when the body will be reconstructed from it. This tradition echoes not only the life force present within the seemingly "dead" earth, but the eternal nature of the human being, created from the dust of the earth.

21. *Sanhedrin* 98a.

22. *Zohar* 2:7a.

23. One of these was the Ba'al Shem Tov. Before his passing, he told his students that had he wanted he could have been like the prophet Elijah and left this world by rising up to heaven in a fiery chariot. Instead he chose to fulfill the verse, "dust you are and to the dust you shall return." His desire to return to dust expressed his deep spiritual connection to physicality.

24. [Editor's note: Interestingly, a report by the San Francisco-based WR Hambrecht & Co. calls Israel "a seat of the global technology world, an incubator of sorts, responsible for producing emerging proprietary technologies that will continue to be important as the telecommunications and information technology industries grow" (*Jerusalem Post*, Dec. 15, 2000, p. 15A).]

25. Accordingly, a Jewish melody has the power to arouse Jewish consciousness and a sense of Divine grace even in a person far removed from his connection to God and Torah. Science, on the other hand, even when revealed by a Jew, does not necessarily remind him of his Jewishness.

26. Rabbi Dov Ber (?-1772), the successor to the Ba'al Shem Tov who was known as the Maggid of Mezeritz, drew upon the metaphor of a male eagle who, to avoid crushing his young, hovers above his nest when feeding them, "touching yet not touching" (*Or Torah* 83; cf. Rashi on Deut. 32:11). The eagle symbolizes God in relation to Israel in particular and to the totality of His creation in general continually withdrawing and concealing His manifest, omnipotent presence and subsequently reasserting it, commensurate with the ability of "finite vessels" to assimilate it.

27. And, indeed, it is taught in Hassidism that in the future, the spirit will be sustained by the body (*Torat Shmuel 5637*, 88 ff; *Sefer HaMa'amarim 5659*, p. 99 ff; *Sefer HaMa'amarim 5666*, p. 528).

# 6. Fifth Dynamic

1. Ecclesiastes 10:1. The simple meaning of this verse as it is usually translated appears to indicate that a little foolishness can negate a lifetime of wisdom and honor. The translation employed here follows the interpretation of the Midrash (*Kohelet Rabbah* 10:1) that at the appropriate times a little foolishness is more precious than both wisdom and honor.

2. The Midrash (cited above) relates:

> *Death-flies stink, yet they ultimately express fragrant oil....* This refers to Korach and his followers. Yesterday they stirred up a foul odor against Moses and said, "Moses is not a true prophet, and Aaron is not the High Priest, and the Torah is not from heaven," and today they...say, "Moses is a true prophet, Aaron is the High Priest and Torah is from heaven."
>
> *...more precious than wisdom, than honor...*: This is [Moses'] prophecy.
>
> *...is a little foolishness*: This is the decree of Moses, as it is written: "but if God creates a new thing..." [Numbers 16:30].

3. Numbers 16:29-30.

4. The above Midrash continues:

> *Death-flies stink, yet they ultimately express fragrant oil...* This is speaking of Doeg and Achitofel. Yesterday they stirred up a foul odor against David and they said, "His family is unfit—isn't he descended from Ruth the Moabitess?" Today they are expressing sweet words and are ashamed.
>
> *...more precious than wisdom, than honor...*: This is the prophecy of David.
>
> *...is a little foolishness*: "and you, God, shall bring them down into the pit of destruction" [Psalms 55:24].

5. See 1 Samuel 21-22; 2 Samuel 15-17; *Bamidbar Rabbah* 18:17; *Sanhedrin* 69b, 106b).

6. The above Midrash continues:

*Death-flies stink, yet they ultimately express fragrant oil...*: This speaks of the generation of Elijah. Yesterday they were stirring up a foul odor and saying things against him: "Ba'al, answer us!" [1 Kings 18:26] and today they are saying, "*God* is God, *God* is God" [*ibid.*, v. 39].

...*more precious than wisdom*...: this is the Torah.

...*than honor*...: this is the prophecy of Elijah.

...*is little foolishness*: "And Elijah took them [the priests of Ba'al] down to the valley of Kishon and slaughtered them" [*ibid.*, v. 40].

7. 1 Kings 18:27.

8. See *Tanya*, Chapter 29.

9. rbs 17:26.

10. Genesis 2:18.

11. In the Talmud (*Nidah* 17a) there is a discussion of the fine difference between a *tzadik* and a *chasid* in the context of how one must dispose carefully of his fingernails when cutting them, lest a pregnant woman come and step on them, causing her to miscarry. A *tzadik*, we are told, buries his fingernails while a *chasid* burns them. The difference is based on another Talmudic statement which asserts that if a person consciously destroys any part of his body it can very negatively affect him. The *tzadik* is careful to bury his fingernails so as not to endanger a pregnant woman or himself. A *chasid* burns his fingernails because even though it may hurt him, he would rather suffer personally than take even the slightest risk of the fingernails being unearthed, thus possibly hurting another.

12. *Likutei Moharan* 1:6.

13. *Sotah* 3a.

14. 1 Samuel 21:14.

15. Psalm 34:2.

16. Ecclesiastes 3:1.

17. *Ibid.* 3:2-8.

18. These 28 times are alluded to as well in another verse: "In Your hand are my times" (Psalms 31:16). The Hebrew phrase word for "in Your hand" (*beyadcha*) can be read "Your two hands" (*beit-yadecha*—because the prefix letter

*beit* equals 2). The numerical value of the Hebrew word for "hand" (*yad*) is 14; thus, "two hands" symbolize the 14 pairs of times (28) that are ultimately in God's hands.

19. Proverbs 24:16.

20. In effect this is an even deeper manifestation of the dynamic of integrating science and other secular knowledge with Torah.

21. Job 20:15. One of the seventy-two three-letter Names of God revealed in Kabbalah appears as the first letters of the phrase "he [evil] has swallowed down riches and he shall vomit them up again" (*chayil bala vayeki'enu*). The power to make evil vomit out the very holiness it has sucked upon derives from this holy Name. Therefore, in prayer books which contain Kabbalistic notations, we are taught to have this Name in our thoughts when reciting the blessing in the *Amidah* for the ingathering of the exiles: "Sound the great shofar for our freedom, raise the banner to gather our exiles and gather us together from the four corners of the earth...." The three letters of this Name of God appear in the second-to-last letters of the words "together from the four corners" (*yachad mei-arba kanfot*).

22. This spiritual law also has a parallel manifestation in the Torah's warning that, if the Jewish people do not follow God's commandments when living in the land of Israel, the land itself will vomit them out (Leviticus 18:28).

23. Exodus 1:9-11.

24. For that reason they will even appear to succeed, as it is taught: "insolence will increase...the government will turn to heresy...the meeting place for scholars will be used for immorality...the fearers of sin will be despised..." (*Sotah* 49b). In general, the situation will express the sages' idiom of "the hour laughing for the evil one's good" (*Berachot* 7b).

25. Had this process been undertaken in the spirit of the Torah, it most likely would have precluded the suffering that did accompany it. It certainly would have precluded this had the Jewish people been consciously inspired by the teachings of the inner dimension of the Torah, about which it is promised in the *Zohar* (3:124b, see *Igeret HaKodesh* 26): "Since Israel will in the future taste of the Tree of Life—which is the book of the *Zohar*—they will go out of exile *in mercy*, and it will be fulfilled in them the verse 'God alone will lead them, without any foreign god'" (Deuteronomy 32:12).

One of the first secular Zionist movements went by the name *Bilu*, the abbreviation of the phrase "O House of Jacob, let us go..." (Isaiah 2:5). Rabbi Shmuel, the fourth Rebbe of Chabad-Lubavitch, commented on this that had they not removed the end of this verse ("...and walk in the light of God"), he himself would have joined the movement and brought with him a hundred-thousand of his followers as well.

26. Based on 2 Samuel 14:14.

27. "A person does not commit a sin unless a spirit of foolishness [i.e. unholy folly] has entered him" (*Sotah* 3a).

28. As demonstrated in the account of how Achish, the king of Gat, threw out (i.e. vomited out) David (1 Samuel 21).

29. *Ketubot* 17a.

30. Rabbah bar Nachmani (270-330 CE) was called "Uprooter of Mountains" (*Oker Harim*, see *Berachot* 64a).

31. 2 Samuel 6:16-23.

32. As it is written: "Serve God with joy, come before Him with rejoicing" (Psalms 100:2).

33. *Mishneh Torah, Lulav* 8:12-13.

34. *Sukah* 5:1.

35. *Mishneh Torah, Lulav* 8:14-15.

36. 25:6.

37. See *Malchut Yisrael,* vol. 2, pp. 195 ff.

38. Ecclesiastes 10:1.

39. Deuteronomy 7:7.

40. *Chulin* 89a.

41. *Shabbat* 118b.

42. *Avot* 4:2.

43. *Nidah* 61b.

44. There are several phases in the process of the nullification of *mitzvot* in the future; at each stage the word "null" takes on a different meaning. The interpretation presented here applies even to what is referred to in Hassidism as

the second, miraculous stage of the Messianic era, even before the Resurrection of the Dead. See *Igeret HaKodesh* 26 (145ab).

45. *Avot* 2:15.

# 7. Conclusion

1. Maimonides explicitly states that the Messiah will not have to perform any miracles in order to verify his authenticity (*Mishneh Torah, Melachim* 11:3).

2. Isaiah 56:7.

3. *Mishneh Torah, Melachim* 12:5.

4. 90:4.

5. Psalms 84:8.

6. This sense is represented in the Talmudic statement: "The sages acknowledged the logic of Rabbi Meir" (*Beitzah* 31b, etc.). Although the sages could barely grasp the intricate and dazzling argumentation of Rabbi Meir, they nonetheless had a sense of his logic's inherent truth and acknowledged it accordingly.

7. *Sanhedrin* 43b.

8. Saadia Ben Yosef (882-942).

9. Deuteronomy 11:13-21.

10. The Hebrew word for "heaven" (*shamayim*) is constructed from the words for "fire" (*eish*) and "water" (*mayim*), elements that in this world are antagonistic yet in their spiritual source are complementary.

The concluding words of the second paragraph of the *Shema* discussed above are: "In order that your days and the days of your children be prolonged upon the land that God has sworn to your ancestors to give them, like the days of the heaven on the earth." The first two paragraphs of the *Shema* allude to the mission of the Jewish people to dedicate themselves through Torah and its commandments to reveal "heaven on earth." These paragraphs further confirm God's promise that a time will indeed come when this idealized reality will actually be realized.

11. Proverbs 3:17.

12. "God looked into the Torah and created the world" (*Bereishit Rabbah* 1:1).

13. This stage corresponds to *kiddush HaShem*, the continual giving of one's life to God.

14. Isaiah 2:3.

# Index